SCIENCE AND CULTURE SERIES

JOSEPH HUSSLEIN, S.J., Ph.D., GENERAL EDITOR

THIS WAY HAPPINESS

THIS WAY
HAPPINESS

ETHICS:
the Science of the Good Life

Charles P. Bruehl, Ph.D.

THE BRUCE PUBLISHING COMPANY
MILWAUKEE

Nihil obstat: JOSEPH A. M. QUIGLEY, Censor librorum
Imprimatur: ✠ D. CARDINAL DOUGHERTY, Archiepiscopus Philadelphiensis

July 5, 1940

Copyright, 1941
THE BRUCE PUBLISHING COMPANY
Printed in the U. S. A.

Ethics

For you see, Callicles, our discussion is concerned with a matter in which even a man of slight intelligence must take the profoundest interest — namely, what course of life is best. (Socrates, in Plato's *Gorgias*.)

Preface

The present volume, offered to college students and the general reader, seeks to unstiffen ethical teaching and recast it in a less rigid mold, thus rendering the subject less solemn and formidable, the reason being that morality is not a matter of mere academic interest but of commonplace work-a-day life. Pursuant to this practical aim it stresses what might be called the lowlier moralities of everyday life which many in their preoccupation with the higher moralities are likely to forget. The practical trend will also be observable in its endeavor to bring home the conviction that morality is not a narrowing influence but that it makes for a richer life and greater happiness. The morally good life is the good life in its most comprehensive and inclusive sense. Morality is neither negation nor frustration but fulfillment. The claim that emancipation from the moral law brings freedom and abiding happiness is a sophism which daily experience rudely shatters.

As the writer sees it, the purpose of ethics is not so much to supply a set of rules for conduct as rather to develop moral sensitiveness which will enable one quickly to appreciate the moral implications of a given situation. Moral insight is the prerequisite of moral conduct. Unless a man is keenly alert to the moral complexion of a situation he cannot respond in the proper manner. If ethical study sensitizes moral perception and renders the mind responsive to the moral import of ordinary occurrences it has accomplished a very valuable function for very often men are not aware of the moral bearings of the circumstances in which they are placed and as a consequence completely fail to get the meaning. The ethically alert man, however, will discover moral issues in all human contacts.

In this connection a strange phenomenon may be pointed out. There exists such a thing as moral color blindness, that is, certain individuals who are quite alive to some forms of moral evil are utterly insensible to others. In fact many conveniently develop blind spots of this kind. Moral color blindness, however, is not congenital but acquired.

The cultivation of a sympathetic imagination is essential to consistent moral conduct. Thus mental cruelty in most cases may be traced to dullness of imagination. The man lacking a vivid imagination has difficulty in realizing the consequences of his actions and cannot place himself in the position of the one who is affected by them. Sympathy does not always get the recognition which it deserves. And for the same reason kindness by many ethicians is accorded only an inferior rank in the scale of virtues. Still the man who carefully avoids inflicting pain and humiliation on his fellow men will rarely become guilty of grave moral lapses.

The author sends forth his ethics in homespun in the fond hope that it will render useful service and justify its existence. He avails himself of this occasion to extend his thanks to Father Husslein for helpful suggestions and encouragement. He also acknowledges a great debt to Father Francis A. McDermott, Professor at the Thomas More Highschool, Philadelphia, Pa., who generously helped in the preparation of the manuscript. Appreciation is also given to the publishers who have granted permission to quote from their publications.

C. BRUEHL

St. Charles Seminary,
Overbrook, Philadelphia, Pa.
Sept., 1940

Contents

PART I
General Ethics

I

Nature and Scope of Ethics

1. THE STARTING POINT OF ETHICS — THE FACT OF MORALITY

Like every other science, ethics has an empirical or factual basis, that is, it finds in the world about us a distinct and definite group of facts which it attempts to understand and explain. In a comprehensive manner these facts or phenomena, which in spite of their apparent superficial variety possess a true unity, we designate as morality or the moral order. Morality presents a real aspect of human life and even as man is born into a physical world so is he born into a moral order, which surrounds him and touches his being at many points. Morality is a fact and as such intrigues man's curiosity and offers reason a challenging problem. This fact of morality constitutes the subject matter of ethics.

Even a little reflection convinces us that morality is not a remote thing but one which confronts us in our everyday experience; it is not merely a fact but a predominant fact which occupies our attention and interest to an absorbing degree. The moral fact imposes itself and refuses to be ignored; sometimes it makes itself felt in a very uncomfortable way; more frequently it is experienced as a friendly and benign influence. It can no more be set aside than the law of gravity. It is of vital importance to the individual as well as society, and hence men everywhere evince keen interest in moral studies.

3

What first gave rise to ethical speculation was the existence of usages and customs (*mores, ethos,* whence the name of the science) which profess to regulate human conduct in a coercive manner, claim for themselves an indispensable authority, demand obedience, are invested with a certain sanctity and enforced by sanctions of various kinds. These customs appear as imperative rules endowed with the character of duties. In the estimation of men, they make for the better life and contribute to the welfare of the community. Conformity to these rules of conduct imparts worth and dignity to human personality and is the reason why men are called good. In turn men look upon these customs with reverence and regard them as binding. Thus morality presents itself as a way of living consonant with human dignity, conducive to the good of society, enjoying social approval, and possessing the form of obligatoriness. That morality in this sense is a fact we learn from sociology.

Morality has impressed itself deeply on our language. Since language is the mirror of life it cannot fail to reflect a fact holding such a commanding place in human existence. Words carrying with them a moral import abound; some are like golden threads woven into the texture of speech, such as justice, right, honor, virtue, duty, devotion, loyalty, heroism, love of country, unselfishness, self-sacrifice, mercy, charity, kindness. Others are sinister in their implications as sin, vice, crime, guilt. Accordingly language bears eloquent witness to the moral character of man.

Evaluation is one of the most characteristic attitudes of man. Expressions of appreciation refer to many things that arouse his interest and appeal to his sense of values. Esthetic judgments belong to this category. The most common and most significant evaluations, however, are moral appraisals. We make a distinction between good and bad actions and, when we apply these qualifications, we have in mind something quite different from physical effectiveness. A burglary job may from the standpoint of efficiency have been executed in an excellent manner and will yet be pronounced bad and viewed with disapprobation. Men set great store by such moral appraisals and very few, indeed, are indifferent to them. This latter fact accounts for the prevalence of hypocrisy, which is mute testimony that even the vicious respect genuine goodness, as La Rochefoucauld pointedly remarks: "hypocrisy is the homage which vice renders to virtue." Even before their own judgment men seek to avoid condemnation and try to justify their doings. This wish to appear good in our own estimation gives rise to the strange device of unconscious self-deception, which the psychologist calls rationalization, and by which we endeavor to disguise base motives and vile intentions. There are things which man will not admit even to himself lest he forfeit all self-respect.

Knowledge of the moral worth of men is of far-reaching consequence in our relations and dealings with them. Indeed, the fundamental question about a man is whether he is good or bad, honest or dishonest, selfish or unselfish. Other matters are of secondary importance. In grouping men, moral goodness is the decisive factor. This is borne out by the general experience of mankind. From the earliest days of our childhood we have learned to make this distinction and our attitudes toward our fellow men are determined by this classification. Moral appraisals either of ourselves or others are often deeply tinged with emotion and evoke strong affective responses.

Moral experience is a reality which it is impossible to deny. We cannot escape the consciousness of obligation and responsibility. We feel the attractive power of virtue and are repelled by vice. At times we are all confronted by the conflict between pleasure and duty. We are deeply convinced that we may not do everything which we could do. There are actions of which we feel ashamed in our innermost hearts though they have brought us no harm and are hidden from the eyes of our fellow men. A feeling of worth results from the performance of certain actions and a depressing feeling of unworth from the performance of others. Men are crushed under the burden of guilt which weighs heavily upon them. A man devoid of any moral scruple would be looked upon as lacking a distinctive human attribute and regarded as a revolting monstrosity. Remorse inevitably follows in the wake of certain deeds. "The wicked flee when no man pursueth" (Prov. 28:1). Conscience will make its voice heard and can neither be silenced nor bribed. Regardless of how we may explain it, the "still, small voice," sometimes so annoying in its admonitions and disconcerting in its reproaches, is a familiar phenomenon. We propose high ideals to ourselves and pursue them with ardor in spite of the fact that our striving calls for great efforts and requires frequent sacrifices. We say that a man has not the right to do a certain thing though he may have the physical power to do it. Vehemently humanity rejects the identification of might and right. There is something which stays the hand even of the most absolute despot.

By certain ties, such as a vow, a word of honor, a promise, a contract, an oath, man holds himself bound more effectively than by a chain of iron. A scrap of paper may become something sacred and inviolable. We are here in presence of something which transcends the physical, and bears witness to an entirely new order of things.

We discover in human history the operation of forces which do not flow from mere selfishness. There is in the world of men a power that makes for righteousness and ministers to justice. The oppressed are not left without champions. Slavery was not abolished by the slaves but by society which saw in it an ugly and hideous thing. Wrongs and abuses are swept from the face of the earth by the aroused sentiment of moral indignation.

We find in this world institutions, such as the family, society, laws, the state, which command the allegiance of men and are held in the highest esteem. Humanity values and protects them. Though they regulate his life in a very drastic fashion, put rigorous restrictions on his personal freedom and impose severe requirements, man accepts them, conforms to their demands, submits to their disciplining restraints and reverences them as something sacred and supremely valuable. Yet they rest not chiefly on coercion but on devotion. Their security lies in their moral majesty. They are upheld and safeguarded not by external force but by the internal loyalty of the race. There is an intangible holiness about them which men spontaneously recognize. "It has been often pointed out," remarks Sir Paul Vinogradoff, "that public order in the broad sense of the word is maintained not by a few policemen, but by the more or less explicit approval of the public at large. The hangman, the policeman, and the soldier would not be strong enough to ensure social order and obedience to law for any length of time if the people at large were not disposed to back them."[1] Hence when moral sentiment no longer supports them, the mightiest empires crumble.

Thus morality proves to be a predominant fact, a wholesome influence, a sustaining force, which enters into the larger part of our actions and into all human and social relations. Life is shot through with moral situations and moral problems crop up at every turn of the road. Morality is the atmosphere in which man breathes. It is the characteristic element in human activity. It does not constitute a sphere set aside from other spheres of activity but rather embraces the whole of human life, so that every situation in life may take on a moral complexion.

The foregoing survey plainly indicates that morality is an actual fact and that moral experience has a very poignant reality. Man, then, is a moral self as well as a physical self. The concept of the moral has a content of its own. It is this uniqueness of the phenomenon of morality which justifies the existence of ethics as a science in its own right.

[1] Vinogradoff, Paul, *Outlines of Historical Jurisprudence*, Oxford Univ. Press, N. Y., p. 92.

Ethics gathers the pertinent facts, shows their mutual relations and reduces them to an orderly system; it clarifies them
and gives them scientific precision. After this it proceeds to
the more important task of ascertaining the nature of morality and its roots or causes.

2. QUESTIONS RAISED AND ANSWERED BY ETHICS

A science consists of answers to questions relative to a
body of similar facts. It will help us to form a clearer notion
of the drift and scope of ethical inquiry if we bring before
our mind some of the questions which grow out of the facts
of morality that have been pointed out.

That morality is a fact cannot be gainsaid, but on closer
inspection does it appear as a reasonable fact, or is it a mere
prejudice to be outgrown? Is it arbitrary and man made or
has it a firm anchorage in the order of the universe? What is
its origin and validity? Somehow morality has to do with the
good life but can we determine the nature of the good life?
Is it a variable quantity or is it absolute in character? Is
there a criterion which enables us to define the good with
certainty? Who is good? What kind of a man ought I to be?
Does it matter whether a man is good or bad? Is it bound up
with significant consequences? Is there any relation between
morality and happiness? What tremendous sanctions give to
morality its supreme importance? May I not simply follow
the path of pleasure? Whither would such a course lead?

This in turn suggests other questions. What is the meaning of life and purpose of human existence? Is there a goal
which man must reach and the attainment of which constitutes for him the highest good? Is there really one thing necessary the loss of which cannot be compensated for by anything else?

The heart of ethics is duty which is manifested and imposed by conscience. We cannot but ask: What is the basis
of duty and the source of its sacredness? What is the author-

ity of conscience and whence is it derived? On what grounds rests the obligatoriness of the law? In the conflict between pleasure and duty, which side must I choose?

Life offers many values and man has a variety of interests. Which of these values and interests enjoy a preferential status? By what standard do we judge values? What is ultimately desirable as associated with our truest interests?

Why must rights be respected? Wherein are rights rooted? Are there inalienable rights of which man may not be deprived?

These questions indicate the wide range of ethics and also its practical bearing. They are not thrust upon us from without but rise in our own consciousness and cannot be suppressed. They are of vital relevancy and an answer must be found. In view of this we readily understand why men have always been fascinated by moral questions, discussed them with passionate concern and devoted themselves eagerly to the study of ethics. A philosophy that does not give a satisfactory account of the fact of morality is barren of human interest and does not deserve the name. This makes Cicero very emphatically say: "Moreover, the subject of this inquiry is the common property of all philosophers; for who would presume to call himself a philosopher, if he did not inculcate any lessons of duty?"[2] The sages of all times concur in the opinion that of all inquiries the most important are those which aim at the discovery of the right and wrong forms of human conduct. The interest evinced is not only academic but exceedingly practical because experience has taught that wrong forms of human conduct, whether in private or social life, result in personal suffering and social misery. In fact it often happens that when a mode of behavior proves injurious or a social condition becomes oppressive they are subjected to severe ethical scrutiny and re-examined in the light of basic moral principles. Moral consciousness sometimes can only be aroused by the painful

[2] *De officiis*, I, II, 6.

consequences of wrong, as is now the case with regard to divorce, birth control, rugged individualism, and war.

3. THE FIELD OF MORAL JUDGMENTS

Morality has to do with actions but it is concerned only with a certain type of activity. The beneficent or destructive operations of nature, subject to the law of mechanical sequence, lie outside the domain of morality as also the impulsive and instinctive actions of animals. Morality is predicated only of beings possessing self-consciousness and capable of reflection. Moral acts are those which are performed with a view to an end, with reference to a standard or rule and are the outcome of a choice. Activity of this kind is designated as conduct to distinguish it from behavior, the quality of which is totally determined by organic structure. Moral conduct is more than reaction to a stimulus or spontaneous response to an object, it implies an awareness of the self as agent, apprehension of an end to be realized, deliberation, and self-direction. It transcends the order of necessary causality and belongs to the realm of ends, purposes, motives, and alternatives which is subject to rational control. Man's actions fall into two groups, those which are performed without advertence and conscious motive and which escape the deliberate control of the agent, and those to which he gives thought, which he directs toward a preconceived end and which it is in his power to do or to omit. The former pertain exclusively to the physical sphere of being and do not become objects of moral evaluation; the latter, however, enter into the moral sphere, that is, they present an element, on the basis of which they may be classified as good or bad; such acts, namely, bear a relation to the rule of reason to which the mind compares them before it decides.

Unreflecting acts do not come under the moral category unless they spring from a deliberately acquired habit or are the expression of character.

The analysis of a moral situation discloses the following

features: a moral situation is characterized by the presence of competing values or antagonistic goods; it confronts us with a categorical imperative, the sign of which is the auxiliary verb ought; it forces a choice on us and takes on the form of a temptation. The possible alternative must be of some consequence. Not unfrequently a real internal struggle is caused by the alternatives involved and to do what one recognizes as the right thing calls for strenuous exertion. It is this common experience which led Dr. W. James to observe in his *Principles of Psychology:* "If a brief definition of ideal or moral action were required, none could be given which would fit better the appearance than this: It is action in the line of greatest resistance." From this we infer that the morally good life is not pleasantly drifting; it means living at high tension and calls for truly manly qualities; in no sense could it be scorned as fit only for the spiritless or weak and effeminate natures. On the contrary, it spells vigorous striving, high-minded endeavor, and sustained courage.

4. THE PREDICATE OF THE MORAL
    JUDGMENT

Moral predicates are applied in the most comprehensive manner. Thus moral goodness is not goodness in any narrow or restricted sense (as when I say, he is good as a mathematician) but that which makes man good simply, absolutely, and in the highest sense. It is that goodness which becomes him as a man, as a human personality, not merely a relative goodness required of him under some special aspect or in some partial and limited capacity. So Aristotle in his *Nicomachean Ethics* asks: "Can we suppose that while a carpenter and a cobbler each has a function and a business, and accordingly also an excellence of his own, man has no business and no function assigned to him by nature?" Moral goodness precisely is that excellence which is due to man by reason of his being man and the absence of which detracts from his worth as a human being and cannot be compensated for by any goodness in a particular field. For this goodness man is destined. It is his fundamental and essential vocation. Its attainment makes him in the truest and fullest sense man. It lifts him to the typical and ideal form of human selfhood. To the extent that he lacks moral goodness he is less a man.

The foregoing brings home the full meaning and force residing in the predicate of moral judgment.

If there is a definite kind of goodness for man this means that he has a definite end, for goodness denotes serviceableness, usefulness for a purpose. The kind of man we ought to be depends on the end for which we exist. Ethical inquiry, therefore, necessarily leads to the investigation of the ultimate end of man, because the good man is he who fits himself for his end and realizes his destiny. Hence F. Paulsen aptly defines the object of ethics when he writes: "It has a double function to perform: to determine the end of life, or the highest good, and to point out the way or the means of realizing it. It is the business of the doctrine of goods to establish the goal, the highest good. The second problem of ethics is solved in the doctrine of virtues and duties."[3]

Many goods and many ends exist which may be freely chosen. But the task of ethics is to prove that there is an absolute good and a supreme end which it is imperative to choose; one which is worth choosing for its own sake whereas all other ends are chosen merely as a means toward the attainment of this one sovereign end. This was the conclusion which Aristotle derived from his analysis of moral conduct and which he states in *Nicomachean Ethics* as follows: "If in all our conduct, then, there is some end that we wish on its own account, choosing everything else as a means to it; if, that is to say, we do not choose everything as a means to something else (for at that rate we should go on *ad infinitum*, and our desire would be left empty and vain); then clearly this one end must be the good — even, indeed, the highest good. Will not a knowledge of it, then, have an important influence on our lives? Will it not better enable us to hit the right mark, like archers who have a definite target to aim at? If so, we must try to comprehend, in outline at least, what it is, and to which of the sciences or arts it belongs."

The pivotal point of ethical investigation is the problem of establishing clearly and convincingly the final end or purpose of human existence and setting forth in strong relief the highest good, because we are likely else to be absorbed in lower ends and rest satisfied with inferior goods and the partial happiness which they afford.

5. ETHOS — MORES

Morality, according to its etymological derivation, has reference to custom and usage. In every social environment we find that certain forms of conduct are generally approved as necessary to a decent human life and conducive to the common good. To be morally good, then, would be the same as to conform to the established customs and accepted usages of society. In a limited sense this is true. A custom coextensive with humanity and reaching down the ages may safely be regarded as good but usages prevailing within different social groups are very often wrong. The mere fact that a custom exists in a given society offers no guarantee that it is right. Professor Theodore de Laguna in his *Introduction to the Science of Ethics* correctly states the matter: "All admit, to be sure, that the mere fact that a condition of affairs exists, or that an act is commonly performed, does not prove it to be right." Accordingly, social customs are not of themselves infallible standards. Prophets and reformers have arisen against custom and tradition, condemned them in the name of a higher law and proclaimed a better way.

In fact, it is the office of ethics to examine critically the existing social codes of conduct. Ethics is more than a descriptive science merely holding up to the present the mirror of the past. In this it differs from sociology which confines

itself to a recording of facts. Ethics says what should be and
sets forth the ideal of which a given custom falls short. It
undertakes the criticism of existing customs and judges them
in the light of principles and norms derived from reason. It
very often questions the validity and challenges the legi-
timacy of accepted ways of living. Its attitude is judicial; it
approves or disapproves; it tries to bring the real into accord
with the ideal.

Now the criterion by which ethics judges existing moral
conditions is not itself derived from experience, but is the
result of philosophical speculation. Ethics, therefore, is not
a purely empirical or factual science; the emphasis must be
placed on deduction. The chief source of ethical truth is
reason, and the ultimate ethical norms are logical conclusions inferred from certain basic rational principles. To
criticize human conduct means to bring it into harmony
with the requirements of reason. Reason, not prevailing custom, must regulate our conduct, though custom in many
cases provides reliable guidance.

On account of its peculiar character ethics is called a
normative or regulative science. It is for the same reason
also practical because it depicts an ideal world which is to
come into being by human activity. It demands action and
reaches into the future. The practical import of ethics is il-
lustrated in the following passage taken from Prof. John S.
MacKenzie's *Manual of Ethics:* "A good painter is one who
can paint beautifully; a good man is not one who can, but
one who does, act rightly. Goodness is not a capacity or po-
tentiality, but an activity. A good painter may decide to
paint no more; but a good man cannot decide to retire from
the life of virtuous activity; or even to take a rest from it.
There are no holidays from virtue."

6. DEFINITION OF ETHICS

At this stage a definition of our subject will prove helpful
since the purpose of a definition is to bring into sharper

focus what is already known in an unsystematic way and to point our further lines of inquiry.

According to Victor Cathrein, S.J., writing in the *Catholic Encyclopedia,* "ethics is the science of the moral rectitude of human acts in accordance with the first principles of natural reason." Whilst this definition indicates that the object of the science is to put order into man's deliberate acts which are not regulated by inherent norms, it does not explicitly express the regulative principle of this order. Hence, it might profitably be amplified to read: *Ethics is that philosophical discipline which by the natural processes of reason establishes the end of man and in relation to this end determines the rectitude of human acts.* Rectitude in this case plainly means their fitness to lead to the attainment of the end.

We are dealing here with rational morality as distinguished from supernatural or revealed morality. The latter rests directly on divine testimony and promulgates the moral law as an expression of the will of God. This law is contained in the Sacred Scriptures and finds its tersest expression in the Decalogue.

It might be argued that, since we are in possession of an authentic and authoritative expression of morality, it would seem superfluous to embark on a laborious quest of what we already know from another and absolutely reliable source. This argument gains added force from the observation that the code of revealed morality is not only complete and adequate, but also superior to any ethical teaching that has emanated from the mind of man. The superiority and greater efficacy of revealed ethics is brought home to us when we compare Christian peoples to those who are guided only by the principles of natural wisdom.

Withal the study of rational ethics is eminently useful even for those who accept the Christian law and should not be neglected by them. In general, it may be said that though faith supplements, it does not aim at supplanting reason.

Reason, like all human faculties, is a gift bestowed by God and should be used to its fullest extent. Moreover, the study of natural ethics serves to reinforce the dictates of revealed law by showing that they are in accord with the requirements of reason and human nature. It will increase our reverence for the revealed law and make us see that there is nothing arbitrary in this law but that on the contrary it promotes human welfare and stands for the highest human values. As a result of such study our morality will become more and more a morality of insight.

The study of natural ethics offers us another advantage inasmuch as it justifies the demands of revealed morality before our own judgment and enables us to defend them when we come into contact with those who are without the light of faith. To these we can prove the immorality of an act only on rational grounds and, hence, must be familiar with the field of natural ethics. To influence the unbeliever for better living, only the appeal to motives belonging to the natural order can prove effective. Incidentally, it may be remarked that natural incentives can very advantageously be enlisted in strengthening those of the supernatural type. Religious persons often affect to despise prudential motives for right living, but wrongly so for they can give valuable assistance, especially at such times when higher considerations have become somewhat dimmed.

7. NECESSITY AND VALUE OF ETHICS

Whereas the animal is guided by sure natural instinct, a large part of man's activity is left to his own decision. Various courses lie before him and he can shape his own life. He is a rational being and therefore cannot but reflect on his conduct. He is time and again confronted by alternatives which force on him the necessity of choosing between competing goods. In his case nature is not always a ready and infallible prompter. He must be his own guide and map out for himself a plan of action. He cannot always satisfy all his interests and must make up his mind as to which he shall give precedence. Even if he so desired, it would be impossible for him merely to drift; even into the most listless life occasions will enter which compel a decision. Now, when decisions are to be made, they should be made on rational grounds and with clear insight into the value of the alternatives.

"Human beings," writes Dom Thomas Verner Moore, "alone of the living things on earth create careers for themselves by a rational view of the possibilities of life, a choice among its many opportunities, and purposive effort to live out life and govern their actions in virtue of a preconceived plan."[4]

If there is a good or a better life, this fact cannot be without acute interest to man and commands his thoughtful attention. True, there is an unreflective morality, which education and social environment impose upon us, but a moment comes when this morality is questioned and its validity must be proved by rational argument. It is then that reflective moral judgment arises and scientific ethics comes into being. Granted, however, that the individual could go through life without reflection and simply accept the standards of conduct socially sanctioned, then at least the community of which he is a member must find for them a rational basis. The child in this respect is symbolic. For a long time it will readily do what it is told to do but a day will inevitably come when, not from any spirit of rebellion but prompted by the inquisitive urgings of awakening reason, it will ask, Why? And so man and mankind may for a time submit unthinkingly to traditional customs but with intellectual maturity comes reflection on the authority of these customs and on their relation to the meaning of life. In no department of life, least of all in that of moral conduct, is man inclined to acquiesce in, and to accept, a mere factual situation. Willy-nilly he must reflect on the facts and

[4] Moore, Dom. T. V., *Principles of Ethics*, J. B. Lippincott Co., N. Y., p. 3.

come to terms with them and with himself. Every normal man seeks the reason of things; he is a philosopher and, especially, a moral philosopher. He must base his practice on some theory. Whilst the animal lives from moment to moment without thought of the future, man cannot live in this haphazard fashion but must chart a course which he will pursue. Thus at some stage of the intellectual development of the individual and the race, naïve and spontaneous morality must become reflective and prove its authority or break down before the onslaught of selfishness and passion. To effect this transition is the task of ethics which substitutes insight and reasoned convictions for blind acceptance.

This critical reflection is hastened when the moral traditions of the community become hesitating and uncertain, when contradictory moral codes arise and moral practice becomes confused. In our days on account of the chaotic confusion in moral ideas and the general weakening of the consciousness of duty, ethical theory, which shows whence morality draws its binding power and in whose name it commands, is more indispensable than ever.

Society stands in need of moral direction if social control is not to degenerate into a mere rule of might. Without moral guidance mankind would plunge into barbarism. Morality creates and preserves civilization. Civilized society is as unthinkable without a moral creed as without a language for only such a creed can give the right orientation to political government and the proper objectives to statecraft. Hence, Pius XII writes in his encyclical, *Summi Pontificatus:* "Before all else, it is certain that the radical and ultimate cause of the evils which we deplore in modern society is the denial and rejection of a universal norm of morality as well for individual and social life as for international relations."

8. HUMAN INTEREST OF ETHICS

Since ethics is concerned with the good life and the means of achieving a worthy human existence it ought to command the keenest interest of all. As a matter of fact, in its widespread popular appeal it is rivaled only by psychology. Practically every newspaper carries a section devoted to the discussion of ethical questions or personal conduct problems. Here young people often seek advice, a fact which shows that life is beset by bewildering difficulties and disturbing anxieties, for which a solution is eagerly sought. Ethical principles are the beacon lights which save men from making pitiful wrecks of their lives. Right moral counsel has prevented many a disastrous failure.

Nevertheless ethics is not properly appreciated by all and very often sadly misunderstood. Too many forget that it is intimately bound up with our happiness and ministers to the finer things of life. For this ethics itself is often to blame. Wrong methods of inculcating morality have done much harm and rendered ethics hateful. Ethics not seldom defeats its own purpose and alienates the sympathy of the student because it shows itself under its most forbidding aspects by assuming an entirely unnecessary austerity. In this respect it shares the lot of religious instruction for both religion and morality have been handicapped by an unfortunate teaching technique which renders the subject taught distasteful.

Morality should not be expounded chiefly as a restraint that is unwelcome but as a directive which envisages our best interests. It must not be viewed as a foe of our pleasures and natural inclinations but as an enemy of debasing pleasures and of degrading tendencies. It should be seen as an ally of that which is best in ourselves. It does not mainly aim at repression but wishes to bring to fullest fruition all that is truly human. If it curbs that which is base it does so in order to free that which is noble. It is no more an impediment to genuine self-realization than a good road is a bar to progress. This truer concept of morality is obtained if ethics emphasizes more the positive and constructive than the negative and restrictive side of moral conduct. After all, the accent is more on doing than on not doing; mere abstention does not constitute goodness. There is ample room for joy, cheerfulness, and wholesome self-expression in the moral life, which is not at all a cramped life. Ethics, therefore, need not frown on everything which is dear to the human heart but often has occasion to encourage the unspoiled inclinations of our nature. True it imposes duties; yet duties themselves, though formidable when first met, do become pleasant and attractive. Some old philosopher has well said: "I slept and I dreamt life was pleasure; I awoke, and lo! life was duty. I acted and behold! duty was pleasure." Moreover, if ethics imposes duties, by way of compensation it also defends our rights and champions our liberties. It throws safeguards around us which ensure peace, undisturbed personal development and freedom from oppression. If we have found our social environment agreeable and helpful, it is morality that has made it so; if we have experienced consideration, kindness, cooperation in dealing with our fellow men, we owe this to the beneficent influence of morality. Especially since Kant, ethics has taken on a somewhat grim and sour mien. The older moralists who looked upon ethics as the science of the good, the worth-while, and the happy life were in this respect more felicitous and more correct than the moderns who unduly stress law and duty thereby obscuring the fact that these things are for the sake of self-fulfillment, the larger freedom and ultimate happiness.

In a democratic country ethics has a very special relevancy. The form of government enjoyed in the United States, for instance, is avowedly based on moral principles and cannot be maintained unless these basic principles continue to enjoy universal recognition and to command unfaltering loyalty. To survive in a world dedicated to the worship of force, democracy needs a deep ethical inspiration, out of which respect for the rights of others and for constituted authority are born. Only moral restraint and self-discipline can prevent liberty from degenerating into license. The true harmony between law and liberty, private interests and the common good can be effected only under a moral rule which removes all arbitrariness from the relations of government to the governed. Nothing but a quickened and enlightened moral consciousness is able to guarantee the continued blessings of democracy.

Thus ethics appears as a friendly science and Dr. Horatio W. Dresser is right when he says: "True ethical teaching drives no one way. Morality was meant to be a thing of beauty, of eager zest and joy, an affair of the fullness of life. If it has not seemed so, the fault lay with the onesided mortals who by mistaken views of human nature and a mistaken method made virtue unpleasant, neglectful as they were of both Greek and Christian ethics at their best."[5]

9. MORAL TRAINING

Ethics being a practical science has some bearing on conduct as St. Thomas remarks: "In speculative sciences the only thing sought is knowledge. In operative sciences the end is operation" (*Ethicorum*, II, 2). This naturally leads to a consideration of the relation of ethics to education. The relation is twofold.

Ethics needs education if it is to exert any influence on conduct for without such assistance the most beautiful ethical ideals would remain barren. Appropriate training can develop moral sentiment, help toward clearer moral discernment, lead to an appreciation of the higher interests in life and make men see wherein true happiness lies. What is good for man is not immediately perceived and may be brought home by proper instruction. Moral tastes, as esthetical tastes, can be cultivated and brought to greater refinement. The example of a noble character is very effective in influencing others for the better. The instruments of moral training have to be derived from experience and a study of human nature.

[5] Dresser, Dr. H. W., *Ethics: Its Theory and Application,* Thomas Y. Crowell Co., N. Y., p. 14.

If ethics is dependent on education, on the other hand it is ethics that gives education full meaning and purpose. Education must teach how to live, not merely how to make a living. If so, it must know what the life becoming a man ought to be; it produces character and helps in the acquisition of habits; consequently, it must know after what pattern character is to be molded and which habits are desirable. To these basic questions ethics furnishes the answers. The ethical ideal is all important in education. Education not guided by ethics is like a ship without a compass. Educational procedure is only one, and the lesser, aspect of education, the more important matter is that of content, import, and goal. Thus F. W. Foerster says: "The study of the ideal of life is the most important auxiliary science of pedagogy."[6] And more explicitly, Jacques Maritain: "Methods, programs, organization, educational technique are, without doubt, important; but they are, after all, merely secondary. First must come the truth to which the teacher should bear witness. In other words, we must first define the ideal of life that is to serve as a guide in the training of the intellect and the development of personality."[7]

Education is bound to prove futile if it is inspired by false ethical ideals, since in that case it cannot provide a proper preparation for life. Many of the evils that afflict modern society may be directly attributed to defects in our educational methods which prevent the formation of sturdy moral character and lead to a breakdown of discipline in home life and society at large.

Still there are many who have but little faith in the usefulness of theoretical moral instruction. Thus a teacher in France, where ethics is taught as a regular subject of the curriculum, is credited with the rather disheartening remark: "My prize man in morals is the biggest knave of the

[6] *Schule und Charakter*, p. 20.
[7] *Philosophy and Education* by Rev. Franz de Hovre, Ph.D., translated by Rev. E. Jordan, S.T.D., Preface, p. vii.

lot." And I am afraid there are many others inclined to echo this discouraging sentiment. Nevertheless we cannot share the pessimistic view that ethical teaching is futile. Of course, formal moral instruction must go hand in hand with appropriate practical training, for, as Professor Dewey has well pointed out, mere teaching about morals is a barren pursuit since in morality the will and the emotions are deeply concerned. But even if knowledge is not virtue, right knowledge is a great help to proper living. We must reckon with the perverseness of the human will which is free and accordingly may act contrary to better insight. Withal, knowledge, though it does not compel, strongly influences the will. A clear visualization of the evil consequences of wrongdoing will act as a deterrent. The moral life has its attractions and the better it is known, the stronger will be its attractive power and the better able will it be to offset the lure of evil. Ethics does supply motives for right conduct which are not without effect, which make the course of duty appear as the better and worthier, and which impart to it an appeal which evil can never have. Unless totally corrupt, human nature does respond to moral motives, since the good possesses an inherent power and beauty to which the normal human being is not insensitive. Apropos is Dr. Alexis Carrel's observation in his book, *Man the Unknown:* "Moral beauty is an exceptional and very striking phenomenon. He who has contemplated it but once never forgets its aspect. This form of beauty is far more impressive than the beauty of nature and of science." Certainly, the teacher must thoroughly understand the art of motivation and know how to link up motives with the natural tendencies, inclinations, and aspirations of our nature.

The belittling of ethical knowledge is ill advised, though it can be understood as a reaction against an exaggerated intellectualism which would make knowledge and virtue identical. Knowledge is not without its effect on practice; the head guides the hand, the intellect the will. Wrongdoing always embodies an error of judgment, and vice and folly are synonymous. When we speak of knowledge in this connection, we mean real insight into the values of life and not merely the memorizing of moral maxims and precepts accepted superficially without any comprehension of their deeper meaning. Whilst moral goodness is chiefly a question of character, habit, and will, it is also one of knowledge. Moral reformation cannot be effected unless a man learns to take a new view of his past and to see it in an unfavorable light. It is ethics which gives this new understanding by a careful analysis of the implications of immorality and thus prepares the change of mind which is the first step to a change of heart.

10.   RELATION   OF   ETHICS   TO   OTHER   SCIENCES

Ethics must have a metaphysical basis and a cosmic background; it cannot be detached from a philosophy of the universe. The end of man depends on what the purpose of the whole cosmic scheme is. If there is no meaning and purpose to the totality of existence, then manifestly there can be no meaning to human existence. If this is not a rational universe, then we need not look for sense and significance in human life. Logically, therefore, ethics comes last in the hierarchy of sciences. It is the crown of the philosophical edifice.

Moral endeavor is arduous and at times calls for strong incentives. The way to moral perfection is long and laborious; we must know whether it will lead to a worth-while goal or whether all moral striving will not finally be doomed to frustration. With grave concern we ask: Will sincere moral effort attain its end and find appropriate reward or not? Are moral values really permanent and who guarantees the reward of goodness? Is reality friendly to virtue or indifferent to good or evil? Is there a final reckoning, a great universal accounting or will all human records be wiped out? With the young man in Heinrich Heine's poem we send our anxious gaze upward to the eternal skies and ask:

> Tell me what is the meaning of man?
> Whence did he come? Whither goeth he?
> Who dwells beyond the golden stars?

If everything eventually comes to naught and man is engulfed in the total wreck of the universe, morality loses its overshadowing value. If the world order has no more regard for man than for an amoeba, morality becomes inconsequential. If the whole universe is governed by unreason and arbitrariness or is the outcome of mechanical forces, the life of man can have no higher purpose and is stamped with futility. Morality, then, is reduced to a matter of expediency or biological usefulness. In the event that man is only temporal, moral values can have none but a transient, ephemeral value. To maintain its unique status and its absolute character, morality must be solidly anchored in reality. It is philosophy only that can supply such anchorage.

What is good for man, what he should strive after, what end he should unwaveringly pursue, what course of conduct he should adopt, must be determined by his nature, his origin, and his destiny. On these problems metaphysics gives us the needed information. The particular branches of philosophy which furnish this basis for ethics are psychology and theodicy. From these two disciplines we borrow the truths that must be the cornerstone of ethics. We do not refer to these truths as postulates because they are not mere assumptions but proved in the sciences to which they belong.

All differences of philosophical opinion ultimately work themselves out in important ethical results. Materialism entails a denial of morality and sensism leads to mere hedonism. Theism, which holds that the universe is ruled by an intelligent, personal, good, just, and benevolent Being, which has brought man into the universe for an exalted purpose, alone fully explains the supreme authority of duty

and offers adequate sanction for the moral law. No satisfying
system of ethics can be framed which does not admit the
Divine Being as the source, the guarantor and the rewarder
of morality. Unrelated to a righteous and holy God, morality collapses. A sound and complete ethics cannot be developed independently of theodicy.

Ethics is also much beholden to psychology, from which
it derives the doctrine of the freedom of the will, the spir-
ituality and immortality of the human soul, and the true
notion of the nature of man. Since ethics is to determine the
good suitable for man, it must have a thorough understanding of his nature if it is not to fall into serious blunders. It
must bear in mind the composite nature of man, consisting
of body and soul, lest it commit the errors of stoicism, mani-
chaeism, and puritanism, which overlooked the bodily side
of man and constructed a moral code suitable to a being
without flesh and blood and devoid of sentiments and emotions, but impossible for a creature endowed with sense,
feelings, and passions. From false concepts of human nature
come that harshness and rigorism which has helped to make
morality discouraging and odious. On such misconceptions
rest the distorted ideals which are unattainable by man and
lead to a suppression of an essential part of his nature, that
may prove physically harmful or cause internal conflicts.
Christian asceticism has avoided the extremes of puritanism
and stoicism, which also mar the ethical system of Kant, who,
while he made virtue sublime, made it utterly unattractive
and impracticable.

Ethics stands in close relation to economics or social economy. Economics deals with human relations, for example, the
employer-employee setup, and it is for ethics to set forth
how certain moral values are to be realized in these relations.
The attitude of man toward the goods of the earth and their
use involves a moral issue. The distribution of the national
wealth must meet the requirements of justice. It has falsely
been maintained that economic activity constitutes an auton-

omous sphere of action, independent of the moral law and governed exclusively by its own laws, such as the law of supply and demand, the iron law of wages. Even a so-called economic man has been set up who responds only to economic motives. The divorce of economics from ethics has been disastrous for human society and has led to our present sorry economic plight. The industrial system, though it unquestionably has also it own specific laws, must withal be included within the all-embracing moral order. Clearly Pius XI states this fact: "For, though economic science and moral discipline are guided each by its own principles in its own sphere, it is false that the two orders are so distinct and alien that the former in no way depends upon the latter" (*Quadragesimo Anno*). If the moral point of view is left out of consideration, wealth may, as Ruskin remarks in *Unto this Last,* really become "illth," that is a veritable curse to society. A happy change in this respect, however, has come about and it is being recognized that ethics and economics must be brought into closer relationship and that the pursuit of wealth must be curbed.

Precisely because ethics is a practical science from which rules for the conduct of life are to be drawn, it cannot ignore historical experience. It cannot legislate in a vacuum. Hence, it depends on sociological research, without which it would be remote from reality and unpractical. We agree with Professor Albion W. Small who writes in his *General Sociology:* "Ethics must consist of empty forms until sociology can indicate the substance to which the forms apply." We would supplement this by adding that while ethics without sociology is empty, sociology without ethics is blind. So we cannot argue about a fair wage until we have found out that a wage system exists, discovered how it works in concrete circumstances, and have gauged the economic possibilities.

It goes without saying that ethics has intimate points of contact with the sciences of law, the administration of justice, legislation, and government.

11. T H E   S T U D E N T   O F   E T H I C S

The study of ethics calls for a special manner of approach. As the science of ethics presupposes the existence of morality, so the study of this science presupposes the presence of moral dispositions in the student. On account of its practical character, it cannot be studied in the spirit of academic and detached aloofness; for such an uninterested attitude the reference to the self of the student and his conduct is too emphatic. Unless it awakens a resonance in the moral nature of the student, ethical teaching will remain sterile. Without an initial capital or fund of good will in the student, ethical theory will accomplish nothing. Where passion is enthroned, reason will have no chance to speak. The desire to escape the practical application will nullify the appreciation of the argument and dim insight into its logical force. An evil will distorts the reasoning processes and shapes them to serve its preconceived designs. He who fears a conclusion thinks timidly and does not dare to follow logic to its bitter end. Not rarely we come across an ethical theory which plainly has been constructed under the influence and in the service of a perverted will. The study of ethics will prove profitless to those who make no effort to discipline their passions.[8]

[8] Cf. Aristotle, *Nicomachean Ethics*, I, 1.

II

The Otherworldly Principle

1. LIFE AND ETERNITY

As God is the key to the right understanding of the human soul, so eternity is the key to the meaning of life. Temporal life centered in itself is to the great majority of men an unsatisfactory and puzzling affair. It does not bear the mark of finality and leaves too much unfinished business. Everywhere there are loose threads which do not fit into an intelligible pattern. Taken by itself, life does not offer inspiration for the highest moral endeavor. To make it understandable it must have a sequel in which its dissonances are resolved into harmony and its incongruities ironed out. Unquestionably, judged by itself without reference to some beyond, this life would not only be vanity but something utterly monstrous. Tennyson in the poem *In Memoriam* well expresses this thought:

> My own dim life should teach me this,
> That life shall live for evermore,
> Else earth is darkness at the core,
> And dust and ashes all that is.

But life is not to be judged by itself: it points to something beyond itself, to some vast finality, to spiritual and eternal destinies, to ultimate triumphs and to fearful failures. Thus the worth of life is increased beyond measure and daily actions are invested with supreme meaning. And in connection with life, morality also takes on an immeasurable meaning.

In the moral scheme it is the individual that counts for he is the moral agent. As a self-conscious person, man himself in some way must be the beneficiary of moral conduct. The eternity, therefore, which gives meaning to life and value to morality is not merely the permanence of the race but the personal survival of the individual. Man is a citizen of two worlds one temporal and one eternal; what he does in the shadowy world of time determines his destiny and place in the eternal world of final reality. This is what we mean by the principle of otherworldliness.

Accordingly, it may be unhesitatingly asserted that no satisfactory system of ethics can be constructed without reference to another world which imparts to moral values their supreme character and affords adequate sanctions for moral conduct. Ideals pale into insignificance if they are not seen in the light of eternity, *sub specie aeternitatis,* and motives are bereft of force if they merely take into consideration goods that pass away with time. A purely worldly morality lacks both inspiration and dynamic motivation. It cannot maintain itself against the fascination of the world of sense with its seductive glamor. The center of gravity of the moral world, if its gravitational pull is to prove effective, must be shifted to the beyond. As mentioned before, the individual is the subject and bearer of morality and, if the individual has no permanence, the value of morality also can only be figured in terms of time. The fortunes of morality are linked with the destiny of human personality. The interests of the moment will tip the scales if you do not throw an eternity on the other side to outbalance them.

Otherworldly morality does not belittle this life because it makes the next life dependent upon the fulfillment of worthy tasks on this earth. In fact it gives temporal existence a tremendous importance because it prolongs the lines of human life into eternity. The two worlds are not unrelated, but a true and logical continuity exists between them. What is germinal in this life comes to full fruition in the next.

Otherworldly morality is also called religious morality since it is religion, as a system of truth, which bears witness to the world beyond. Improperly it is referred to as clerical morality because the clergy are the exponents of religion. Its counterpart which seeks the foundations of morality exclusively in this life and repudiates all sanctions except the natural consequences of the act, is known as naturalistic, secularistic, positivistic, independent, or lay morality.

The advocates of independent morality, though their avowed aim is to reconstruct morality in conformity with experience, are strangely devoid of a sense of realism and apparently ignorant of the difficulties involved in moral striving, and blind to the allurements of sensuality. They have obviously never gauged the demoniac power of passion and the momentum of selfishness. Familiarity with man's impotence when wrestling with a mighty temptation would shatter their shallow optimism. If not braced by higher spiritual motives, man succumbs to the impact of selfish interests. Those who think otherwise, either underestimate moral ideals or overrate the actual state of man. Their philosophy betrays but scant knowledge of the normal human self and its tragic weakness; it is out of touch with the stubborn facts and moves on the plane of the abstract. The only practical, realistic, scientific and psychological ethics is that which links morality to religion and centers it in the life to come.

2. ETHICAL CULTURE

The most popular form of moral secularism is ethical culture. This movement is identified with a nonreligious morality and holds that morality can and should be maintained and cultivated on its own terms, free from external sanctions or religious motives. Its aim is "to assert the supreme importance of the ethical factor in all relations of life apart from any theological or metaphysical considerations."[1]

[1] Society for Ethical Culture of New York, *Directory*, 1920.

The first society for ethical culture was formed in New York in 1876 by Felix Adler. Its purpose was to provide a center for persons who had lost their attachment to the traditional creeds but desired to foster the moral development of the individual and society. The movement is not hostile to religion but wishes to provide sources of moral inspiration for all classes whom the Churches and Synagogues have ceased to influence. Hence without affirming any creed, it teaches that moral ends are supreme above all other human ends and interests and that the authority of the moral law is immediate and not dependent on religious beliefs or philosophical theories. It thinks that, without religious motivation, it is able to promote appreciation and understanding of the sense of duty, to inculcate respect for the moral law and to inspire reverence for the surpassing dignity and the intrinsic holiness of man.

The aim of the movement is laudable and the ideals for which it stands are lofty but it can have no value for the many who need sturdier motives than those which Ethical Culture supplies.

P. J. Proudhon (1809–1860) tried in a similar manner to build an imposing moral edifice on shifting sand as the following passages indicate: "Completely self-sufficient, ethics must dissociate itself from religion and philosophy. The principle of morality must be sought in a fact of experience revealed in the consciousness of each individual. This interior fact is the spontaneous sentiment which every man has of his personal dignity and the inviolability of his nature. Respect human dignity in yourself and others, that is the foundation of morality and of duty" (*De la Justice dans la Révolution et dans l'Eglise*).

Quite so. The worth of the individual and the dignity of the human personality are truths of basic importance in ethics but they are not immediately evident, they become apparent only when man is conceived of as a creature, reflecting the glory of his Maker, and endowed with an eternal

THE OTHERWORLDLY PRINCIPLE 33

destiny. Patently, the inherent nobility of man was not evident to H. G. Wells when he contemptuously spoke of man's life as "this little stir amid the slime, a fuss in the mud." The dignity of man lies in this that he is from God and for God, a truth which reason must establish.

3. RELIGION AND MORALITY

Religion supports moral effort because it brings out in bold relief those truths which assure the validity of our moral ideals and their ultimate triumph in the universe. It is religious belief that imparts warmth, vitality, and enthusiasm to morality. Without faith in God, eternal justice, and immortality man would weaken in the struggle for righteousness and look upon it as a losing fight. Religious hope, however, reinvigorates the faltering courage and the wavering purpose. The fear and hope of the hereafter have always proved powerful motives for the observance of the moral law. Nothing so effectually checks wickedness as the vivid thought of the future judgment.

4. RELIGION AND MORAL EDUCATION

The erroneous supposition that practical morality can be achieved independently of religion has led to a corresponding false view of mōral education and the exclusion of religious teaching from our public schools. There is now a growing conviction that moral training dissociated from religion falls short of the desired results and fails to produce the highest type of citizenship. To bar religion from moral education means to deprive oneself of the strongest motivation of moral conduct and to surrender the most effective factor in character building. Moral precepts based on abstract reasoning or on a mere analysis of the natural outcome of conduct make but little appeal to the mind of the child. Duty to be impressive will have to take on the concrete form of a divine command and the sanctions of the moral law must be expressed in a manner suitable to the comprehension of the young. It is religion which gives morality this concrete form, clothing it with sacred inviolability.

A recent study of the situation terminated in the following conclusion: "It would therefore seem that there is a
very distinct place for religion in the education of our children, and that our public schools must undertake the rudiments of such education unless we are to remain satisfied
with turning out a large proportion of our youth quite uninstructed in those principles which make for the best
citizenship."[2]

In ethics as well as in moral education God is indispensable. Theistic ethics makes morality a matter of personal loyalty of man to God. Introduced into moral education, this personal relationship makes morality both teachable and lovable. Out of it grow reverence for duty, respect
for the authority of the moral law, a deep conviction both of
the necessity and the beauty of living virtuously. It is useless
to teach the manifold duties of life before a profound sense
of reverence for duty itself has been awakened. Such respect
can be inculcated only if duty be traced back to God, its
ultimate source. To ignore God in moral education means
to leave it on an uninspiring level and to deprive it of the
most dynamic driving force.

Men, therefore, who have not been imbued with a religious world view and whose conscience does not interpret
the dictates of the moral order as the commands of a Supreme and Holy Lawgiver, are seriously handicapped in the
struggle for moral uprightness and integrity. Accordingly,
the best interests of the growing generation are not served
by an exclusion of religion from education for religion is
not a hindrance and a burden but a source of moral strength
and alacrity. Those who practice morality without faith in
a future life are haunted by a sense of defeat and take refuge
in a proud defiance of a pitiless fate and a wearisome resignation to the inevitable.

[2] *The Essential Place of Religion in Education.* Monograph published by
the National Education Association, 1916.

III

The Sovereign Good

1. MORAL GOODNESS AND HAPPINESS

That an intimate nexus exists between moral goodness and happiness is a practical conviction of mankind which finds its expression in many popular maxims. Virtue leads to happiness and vice terminates in disaster. The safest road to travel is that of moral integrity; the transgressor comes to grief and lives to regret bitterly his evil deeds. It is merely a question of time until conscience catches up with the sinner; he may run furiously but will lose the race. But men hold moreover that this corresponds to the eternal fitness of things and that it ought to be so in a rational world; they feel tempted to indict the moral government of the universe when they see the vicious enjoying undisturbed prosperity and the virtuous oppressed and reduced to misery. Thus W. Wundt in his *Ethical Systems* declares: "It would be intolerable to suppose a permanent conflict between happiness and the good." In fact, if opposition between goodness and happiness should prove to be a cosmic drift, our sense of justice would be outraged and reason baffled, human life would appear a grotesque farce and sardonic joke, the world would take on hideous, gorgonean features, freezing the blood in the veins of men and quenching the last spark of moral enthusiasm. Even Kant, who in *Fundamental Principles of the Metaphysic of Ethics* extolls duty for duty's sake and banishes from the sphere of morality every other motive but

35

that of disinterested reverence for the law, is appalled at the spectacle of victorious vice and exclaims: "The sight of a being who is not adorned with a single feature of a pure and good will, enjoying unbroken prosperity, can never give pleasure to an impartial rational spectator. Thus a good will appears to constitute the indispensable condition even of being worthy of happiness." Unless destitute of moral feeling we all share this sentiment and regard the wicked as undeserving of happiness and we are puzzled at the success which attends a nefarious enterprise. Happiness is the right of the morally good. Man is possessed of an ineradicable craving for happiness and if morality were totally irrelevant to this basic desire it could have no interest for man.

We must, however, be careful not to construe the above after the fashion of popular melodrama which ends in the confusion of the villain and the vindication of persecuted innocence. Nor must it be interpreted in the superficial sense of a Polyanna optimism which pictures life in roseate colors. Happiness and goodness are not irreconcilable but the reconciliation does not lie on the surface. It is to be borne in mind that inspiring biographies are not those of happy people. We do not advert to the happiness of the men we honor, we are concerned with their noble deeds, their devotion to high ideals, their loyalty to a great cause, their self-sacrifice, their services to their fellow men, their righteousness, their incorruptibility. With regard to the men and women whose biographies remain unwritten the same observation holds, we respect them for their qualities not for their happiness. Happiness taken by itself compels no moral esteem.

2. HAPPINESS SUBORDINATED TO GOODNESS

Moral striving cannot simply be identified with the seeking of happiness though it is quite true that goodness will be crowned by happiness. Thus whilst happiness cannot be separated from goodness, it is not happiness which intrinsically constitutes goodness. On the contrary, because goodness is what it is in its own right, it brings happiness in its wake. Goodness has a value independent of any consequences which flow from it. Truly, because we recognize in virtue something fine we feel that it merits happiness as its proper reward. Yet virtue is more than a mercenary desire for happiness. Man may legitimately and laudably seek happiness but he must seek it with due dependence on goodness. He who seeks happiness within the moral order, implicitly acknowledges the superiority of this order and pays tribute to it. He is not actuated by naked egotism and pure selfishness but animated by a love of virtue and reverence for the law. On the other hand, the unregulated pursuit of happiness for its own sake would quickly degenerate into gross sensualism and mere pleasure seeking. Witness hereof is the immoral use made of the so-called right to happiness. This false principle is called on to justify divorce, marital infidelity, extramarital sex relations and other perverse practices. Happiness is not an unconditional right but must be merited.

The morally good must never be made contingent on anything else, and a will disposed to do wrong if no evil results ensued would be out of tune with the moral order. Theistic ethics safeguards the supremacy of the moral good because it makes the holy will of God the source of obligation. Hence the acquisition of moral perfection is the fulfillment of a task imposed by God, which has purpose, meaning and worth in and by itself although it necessarily brings happiness.

It is not doing justice to virtue to say that it is nothing more than a striving for happiness. Vainly would one attempt to prove that altruistic conduct is motivated only by regard for the agent's happiness. Such conduct is frequently pursued in outright contempt of personal happiness and at the cost of great sacrifice. The good man lives a life of service, altruistic abnegation and self-surrender. His last thought is of happiness. His will is dedicated to a good of absolute value. His life rises to the plane of the heroic.

In fact, happiness as commonly understood is to be viewed with distrust as long as we are journeying on this earth. The mood of self-satisfaction and complacency which it induces is not particularly helpful in the moral life, which should ever be an outreaching to farther goals. Man here on earth finds himself ever in the presence of the insidious temptation to rest contentedly on lower levels of happiness. The siren's voice of pleasure ceaselessly invites him to abide. Accordingly, the inborn desire for happiness requires ethical orientation for it frequently turns to objects by which it will be thwarted. Too often men are deluded by the apparent good. It is the office of ethics to shatter these delusions, to keep the innate urge at a high pitch of tension and to regulate and discipline the pursuit of happiness by pointing out the objects in which it is to be found. To seek happiness has no moral value but to seek it in the right manner and in the right objects is truly moral. The hour of attainment does not arrive during man's earthly pilgrimage. The moment to which man would say with Faust, "Remain! for now my happiness is complete!" may not come in this world. It would be the end of moral striving.

3. THE   END   OF   MAN

At this point it has to be shown that the end of man does not lie within the narrow confines of time; if this were the case he would be satisfied with this earth and reach within it the consummation of all his desires. Experience teaches the contrary and hence we conclude that earth does not embrace the objects that answer to man's deepest cravings. He is made for something else. His destiny cannot be a merely terrestrial and temporal one, unless we subscribe to the proposition that all human striving, especially that of a nobler character, is purposeless and vain — a proposition which in *Nicomachean Ethics* Aristotle terms monstrous: "Universal failure such as that would be a monstrous anomaly, seeing that there is no impulse of nature that is in vain."

We distinguish between the subjective and objective end. The subjective end is a state of well-being, satisfaction, and happiness resulting from the attainment of a good which in its turn constitutes the objective end. Wants, desires, tendencies point to objects in which the former find fulfillment and rest. When the proper object has been obtained desire ceases. The ultimate end or the highest good would satisfy all desires and confer supreme happiness. It would bring quiet possession, peaceful enjoyment, and be free from torturing restlessness. The craving exists that it may lead us to its object. When the right object has been secured, the craving, having fulfilled its purpose, no longer goads us on. The desire of the human heart for perfect happiness is to lead man to the supreme good. The completion of this desire would indicate that man has come into the possession of this good. But as long as man breathes the craving endures; he finds not what he seeks; the unattainability of perfect happiness in this life, accordingly, shows that the true object of man's quest is not among the goods of this earth. His hunger for happiness, unsatisfied in this world, has the manifest purpose of leading him to another world where the reality exists that will crown all his desires.

4. MAN'S RESTIVENESS, AN INDEX OF IMMORTALITY

In a way it may be said that the earth treats man unkindly, denying him both the happiness which he desires and the perfection of which his faculties are capable. The noblest being on earth is the most unhappy and the most disappointed. The very endowments that elevate him above the animal, reason, reflection, self-consciousness, and a will of limitless range, are the cause of his paradoxical plight. In a world governed by design, this can only mean that what is withheld from him in his mortal days awaits him beyond the grave. Thus Kant holds that the supreme good can only be realized in eternity and on condition that man is immortal: "The *summum bonum,* then, practically is only possible on the supposition of the immortality of the soul; consequently this immortality, being inseparably connected with the moral law, is a postulate of pure practical reason."[1] Even the pagans held that human life must have a sequel if it is to make sense and offer any semblance of completeness. Because for Aristotle the highest good is a thing of time it remains precarious and accessible only to a few.

This life is not the whole life of man. It impresses the thoughtful observer like a jigsaw puzzle in which the key pieces are missing and which, therefore, cannot be fitted together. It has also been likened to the reverse side of a tapestry which gives no hint of order or design.

When a being has attained its end, it rests and finds therein the consummation of all its tendencies, with an attendant state of well-being. For a rational being this means an activity which comes to its fullest fruition by embracing the highest object of which it is capable. This object, the compassing of which crowns all the desires of man and brings about the fullest blossoming of his nature, is never within man's reach during this life.

The test is this. As long as man experiences the torture of unfulfilled desire, as long as his heart is agitated, as long as fear tugs at his heartstrings, as long as uneasiness pursues him, as long as he yearns and painfully strives, as long as he feels himself goaded on, he has not found that for which he exists. Poets and philosophers are one in proclaiming that man does not find his happiness on this earth. To his last breath he remains dissatisfied. Disillusionment dogs his every step. He wearies of the desirable things of life more quickly than a child of its toys. Some objects may confer a keen temporary enjoyment but they quickly pall. Everywhere disenchantment lurks. If we survey the things which men greatly

---

[1] *Critical Examination of Practical Reason,* I, 2, 2, IV.

prize, such as wealth, health, beauty, pleasure, honor, power, position, knowledge, friendship, social prestige, fame, love, virtue, we readily discover that they fail to give permanent satisfaction. They are mostly unsatisfactory in themselves, mixed with evil and treacherous. The unsatisfactoriness of life is a commonplace; it is so evident and so oppressive that man seeks an escape from reality in art and in his dreams. The inadequacy of this life, the vanity and futility of worldly goods has inspired the dreary and cheerless creed of pessimism.

Tersely Everet Dean Martin describes man's sublime discontent with the world in which his brief days are cast: "Other things in nature are complete; they are what they are; we are not. We must find escape and compensation where other living things are content with reality. Reality for us is but half hospitable."[2]

This desire for complete happiness is not a morbid condition but planted in man to urge him on to greater perfection. It grows with mental development. It is the mainspring of the noblest achievements, of the bravest heroism and of the finest loyalty to duty. It truly leads upward. It is natural to man because it is the logical outcome of the infinite sweep of his reason which is bounded by no earthly horizons. Unless the scheme of things is hopelessly awry, in some manner provision must be made for the satisfaction of this intense craving which in the best of the race reaches its highest degree. Fulfillment must be sought in another world where man attains to his true stature. There is no reason why man's existence should be confined to the short span of this life. He is capable of envisioning another life which will compensate for the shortcomings of this one and right its wrongs. Another life is the only acceptable solution since this is a rational cosmos governed by design and benevolent purpose. There the perfect good resides, the striving after which here has been man's chief torment but also the mo-

---

[2] *The Mystery of Religion*, p. 337.

tivating power of all moral progress. Except for the life to come this world would be a senseless treadmill.

This life, then, is only part of a larger whole and gains its meaning in relation to the whole. If seen in this relation, its seeming contradictions and incoherencies vanish and everything is resolved into an intelligible pattern.

5. RELATIVE CHARACTER OF THIS LIFE

This life has no final character. It calls for another chapter to give it a satisfactory ending since it leaves everything in suspense. It does not settle all questions. It is plain that nothing is really brought to an issue unless there is a continuity and proportion between this life and the next, which is the case only when the quality of this life determines the quality of the next, that is, when every man, in his own person and in his own identical and surviving self, albeit as a disembodied spirit, reaps in eternity what he has sown in time. Hence, man obtains his complete happiness if his temporal life has been of a moral quality to warrant such a felicitous outcome. The attainment of ultimate happiness is predicated on one condition: a life worthy of happiness. Accordingly, this life takes on a probationary character, the future to be decided by the judgment of God on the moral value and tendency of the present. Man shapes his own destiny as truly becomes a responsible agent endowed with the power of knowledge, free decision, and self-determination.

This life is an active preparation for the life to come and, therefore, does not mean that we just mark time and passively wait until we enter into our eternal inheritance. Rewards must be earned and do not just drop into our laps as an overripe fruit falls from the tree. Still, while life may not be looked upon as a matter of irresponsible personal enjoyment and self-gratification, it need not be a time of misery and dreariness unrelieved by any bright ray of happiness. In most cases, the moral life even here on earth brings a generous, though not full, measure of happiness. But we cannot say that this life under all circumstances owes us an uninterrupted series of delightful days. After all, life is a way, and the chief purpose of the way is to bring us to our destination, even though it be over rough spots. The way may be pleasant but the pleasures of the way are incidental and not sought for their own sake, for otherwise we would loiter and never reach the destination.

If, however, we wish to assign a proximate end to this life it can be none other than the faithful fulfillment of duty. Duty is the primary purpose of this life. If happiness comes in the wake of duty, it is to be gratefully received. Happiness, however, may not be sought apart from duty.

6. THE OBJECT OF PERFECT HAPPINESS

On account of the unlimited reach of his rational power, the object to give man perfect happiness must itself be limitless. It must be the fullness of truth, goodness, beauty, and every conceivable perfection. This is God, who is the plenitude of being. In Him unalloyed happiness can be found. It will be found in communion and fellowship with the Supreme Being, who is not impersonal but a personal Self and will be to us Father and Friend. With Him and all the good, man will live in a blessed community in which eternal harmony prevails and into which no disturbing shadow can fall, because it is centered on Him who is the source of all good, infinite, changeless, and everlasting. Perfect happiness will be ours when God, for whom we are made, becomes for us all in all.

Since God is the highest term of our faculties, to possess Him does not mean a state of inert rest — but the most perfect form of rational activity, that activity which is typical and distinctive of man. It is the blissful contemplation and love of the Deity, whose glory can never be exhausted by any finite being, and, hence, is the unfailing source of never-ending ecstasy.

The sublimest attribute associated with the Godhead is

holiness, and it logically follows that the only way that can
lead man to the possession of the thrice holy God is holiness
of life. Happiness and holiness cannot be separated; such a
separation would degrade happiness and make holiness
meaningless for man. In the moral universe they are inseparably connected for the moral order prescribes that
course of conduct which leads to perfection and consequently
to happiness because happiness is the natural outcome of a
being living in conformity with its innermost tendencies.

Thus are linked together the highest values of which man
can conceive: morality, duty, perfection, happiness, holiness,
and God. God is central. Everything radiates from him and
converges toward Him. The end of creation is the glory of
God. God's honor is to be known, loved, and served. These
very things also constitute man's perfection and happiness.
Kant expresses this harmonious relation as follows: "Therefore those who placed the end of creation in the glory of God
have perhaps hit upon the best expression. For nothing glori-
fies God more than that which is the most estimable thing
in the world, respect for His command, the observance of
the holy duty that His law imposes on us, when there is
added thereto His glorious plan of crowning such a beautiful
order of things with corresponding happiness. If the latter
(to speak humanly) make Him worthy of love, by the former
He is an object of adoration."[3]

7. DIGNITY OF MAN

The dignity of man will have to be the measure of his
conduct. A low conception of man's inherent worth entails
a low idea of his duties and responsibilities. There is no
better guide in morals than a proper appreciation of human
personality and reverence for its spiritual nature. The sense
of dignity, which is the expression of his spiritual personality
and bears testimony to the rational self behind the self of
sensuousness, calls him to a higher life and will be the reg-

[3] *Op. cit.*, II, V.

Apr. 20 Lindsey 9

Christopher Scheur
574 6th Ave S.W
ND
Dickinson

701-227-1930

carpenter of priest

CARDINAL MUENCH SEMINARY

100 35TH AVENUE N.E., Fargo, ND 58102

GRAND CARNIVAL

Sunday, February 1, 1998 – 12 noon to 5:30 p.m.

Raffle • Food • Auction • Games • Book Sale

1st Prize	**$1000 Cash**
2nd Prize	$ 800 Cash
3rd Prize	$ 400 Cash
4th Prize	$ 200 Cash
5th Prize	$ 100 Cash

Need not be present to win
Drawing Time 5:00 p.m.

$1.00 Donation
City of Fargo Permit No. BR0081-97

5383

ulative principle of his actions. It will help him to rise superior to the imperious demands of animal appetites and carnal passions.

The preceding chapter gives us an inkling of human dignity as it tells us that man has a destiny which transcends time, that he exists for God, that his innate desire for perfect happiness lifts him above all other creatures that roam the earth and eloquently proclaims that he belongs to a better and finer world. His citizenship in the spiritual world will not allow him to become enslaved by the world of sense.

8. THIS WORLD

Though not final in character, this world should realize within the limits of time the ethical good and body forth the moral order. The world should be the kingdom of God, the reign of the moral law, and the embodiment of justice. That is mankind's vocation during this life to make this world a moral world which is favorable to virtue and helpful to honesty. Civilization and culture are to be expressive of spiritual values and shaped after a moral pattern. The rule of social justice must be established. Looking to the next world must not let us neglect the tasks we have in this world. Not flight from the world but cooperation in the moral betterment of the world must be our motto. To the extent that morality prevails in this world, it reflects the glory of God, promotes the well-being of the human race and renders the attainment of the supreme end easier for all. Instead of making us unconcerned about the plight of the world and indifferent to its affairs, otherworldly morality enjoins on us the duty of taking an active part in human advancement and the progress of civilization and of seeing that they move along the right lines. Active interest in the moral transformation of the world is the natural corollary of man's social nature.

It has been falsely contended that otherworldly, notably Christian, morality engenders hostility to cultural pursuits and proves an obstacle to the progress of material civilization. The truth is that Christian moral teaching has actually shown itself to be a ferment of genuine progress and a dynamic factor in human uplift. The otherworldly outlook, however, does prevent men from becoming unduly absorbed in material preoccupations and enables them to maintain a wholesome and well-poised attitude of independence with regard to the goods of the world. The prospect of living eternally in a happy fellowship of mutual love with God and our fellow men will beget toward our fellow mortals here on earth a tender sympathy and an active desire to assist them in every possible manner that, with us, they may attain to this glorious consummation.

IV

The Moral Agent

1. ANALYSIS OF MORAL RESPONSIBILITY

The ideas of morality and responsibility are correlative. By a moral agent, therefore, we understand a responsible person, that is an individual to whom his actions are imputed as a matter of praise or blame, as a title to merit or a cause of demerit. It is important to determine by which acts man incurs responsibility and what precisely constitutes accountability or under what conditions deeds redound respectively to the credit or discredit of the doer. Now it is quite certain that we do not judge all man's actions in this manner and that to many of his doings we attach no moral significance. Only to a very definite kind of act do we apply the moral category and designate them as good or bad, meritorious or demeritorious. The acts classified as moral emanate from man in a special manner and present certain well-recognizable features. We feel that a man cannot be held accountable for what he does entirely from physical compulsion or in a state of unconsciousness.

Responsibility is verified in what are known as human acts. These are so named because they are performed in a characteristically human manner, bringing into play reason and free will, which differentiate man from the brute animal. Man acts as a moral agent when he acts in the capacity of a conscious, knowing, and free self, which has control over what it is doing. Thus St. Thomas says: "Those acts are

47

called human of which a man is master, and he is master of his actions in virtue of his reason and his will."[1] Common sense forbids us to place responsibility on a man for what he cannot help.

The essential condition of moral responsibility and the indispensable attribute of a human act is voluntariness. The quality of voluntariness implies the following:

1. The agent must be conscious of what he is doing and knowledge must initiate or prompt the act;

2. The agent is aware of the end to which the action tends and directs his activity in a purposive manner;

3. The agent controls the act and is free to do or not to do it;

4. He possesses some appreciation of the moral bearing of the act.

The human act being free involves a choice and thus requires a reasonable consideration of the merits of its alternative. Hence we speak of a deliberation which precedes the act of choosing. This deliberation, however, need not be a long drawn-out process; it may be accomplished in a moment and in a flash illumine the situation. There enter, then, into the human act, knowledge, advertence, control, direction, and freedom, and these constituent elements are embodied in the following definition: a human act is an act which proceeds from the deliberate free will of man. It can readily be gleaned from the foregoing that a human, a moral, a free, a voluntary, and an imputable act are synonymous terms. To the extent that the factors mentioned are absent the voluntary character of the act is impaired. Such impairing interferences are quite frequent in everyday life. We refer here merely to inadvertence, which unfortunately occurs very often, owing to man's inability to keep his attention for any length of time at a high pitch.

Only human acts, proceeding from my will freely acting on a deliberate judgment, can truly be said to be my own

[1] *Summa Theol.*, I, II, q. 1.

and consequently carry with them imputability and responsibility. Only such acts can shape our moral personality. That which we do knowingly and willingly makes or mars us. We are what our human acts make us for in them the will expresses itself. Nothing is so much our own as our will and only what we will makes us good or bad. Acts of this type recoil on the self and leave it better or worse. In this sense what Kant says is true: "Nothing can possibly be conceived in the world, or even out of it, which can be called good, without qualification, except a good will."[2]

Since only human acts can make us good and these are our very own and in our power, it follows that moral worth depends on ourselves. It is achieved and not dependent on circumstances, but on our own actions. It is that which is most personal. No one can live our moral life for us; it must be self-conducted by reflection and deliberate choice, not as that of the animal which is the result of blind and uncriticized impulse. True, man also experiences the uprush of impulses and is played upon by the influences of his environment but he can become the master of his impulses and triumph over his environment. A single central purpose can unify his life and dominate the present and the future, and his will can direct all his actions toward one supreme end.

2. WHAT LESSENS THE VOLUNTARINESS OF A HUMAN ACT?

Since man is not a pure spirit but has also a sensuous nature with appetites and tendencies of its own, the exercise of his higher faculties is often obstructed and impeded by influences emanating from this lower phase of his being. Whenever this happens, he acts less as a man and the imputability and responsibility attendant on his act are proportionately diminished. Now, as knowledge and deliberate choice characterize the human act, whatever lessens knowl-

[2] *Fundamental Principles of the Metaphysic of Ethics,* translated by T. Kingsmill Abbot, 1.

edge or reduces the share which the will has in the action, to the same degree also detracts from the perfection of the voluntariness and the human quality of the act. The factors which deprive in a greater or lesser degree an act of its distinctly human character and correspondingly decrease responsibility are ignorance, passion, fear, violence, habit, fatigue, disease, an inherited disposition.

Ignorance is the absence of pertinent knowledge. It may be invincible, when the agent is not aware of it and consequently can take no steps to remove it. It is not, then, culpable. It becomes culpable when its presence is known but the agent for some reason is disinclined to do anything about it; he may prefer not to know his duties lest they become too urgent or he may simply be too lazy to seek information.

What is done through and in inculpable ignorance is involuntary, since the will has no part in it for nothing is willed but what is known. Thus, if I hand to a friend a cup of what I think to be pure wholesome water but with which poison has become mixed in a way of which I have no knowledge, the resulting poisoning of my friend cannot be imputed to me because it is totally unintentional on my part and really against my will. It is a deplorable accident but in no sense a crime. My ignorance of the presence of poison in the case was invincible since there was nothing to arouse a suspicion which might have led to an investigation. Ignorance of this kind removes all responsibility and exonerates from all guilt. A man may happen to do what he does not will (injure another with a gun he thinks is not loaded) but he cannot will what he does not know, and guilt cannot be incurred without will. What is done in consequence of a blameless defect of knowledge is said to be done in good faith. The plea of inevitable ignorance must not be lightly used in self-justification for man has a duty to proceed circumspectly and with forethought in his actions.

There are varying degrees of culpable ignorance: the

simple ignorance of carelessness, the crass or supine ignorance of gross negligence and the studied ignorance of a wicked will. As an illustration of ignorance due to indolence we may cite the incompetence of a physician who failed to prepare himself properly for his professional duties and who as a consequence endangers the health and lives of his patients; it stands to reason that such ignorance which could and should have been dispelled by diligent application makes the agent responsible for blunders in his practice. Studied ignorance is even worse because it is premeditated and deliberatedly fostered in order to serve as an excuse of wrongdoing. It has its source in a will inclined to evil and cannot absolve the agent from responsibility. Whenever there is implicit or explicit acquiescence in ignorance, the latter becomes blameworthy.

Common forms of ignorance are inadvertence and forgetfulness, both of which have their roots in man's natural limitations. Still these distracting tendencies must be combated. The more serious the matter is, the more does it call for earnest concentration. While driving a car it would be wrong to take one's attention off the job in hand and engage in frivolous distractions. Similarly we must guard by all reasonable means against forgetfulness, which may have very grave and annoying consequences.

As a constructive rule it may be laid down that man is bound to acquire that knowledge which enables him to discern his duty in the ordinary circumstances of life and to discharge properly the various tasks associated with his calling. Too often ignorance is illegitimately used as an excuse. To forestall such abuse, civil courts do not recognize ignorance as a sufficient defense, since every man is presumed to be acquainted with the laws of the realm. The law says: "Every man must be taken to be cognizant of the law; otherwise there is no saying to what extent the excuse of ignorance may not be carried."[3] Aristotle holds the same view: "Nor

[3] Cf. H. Campbell Black, *A Law Dictionary*.

is involuntariness predicable of ignorance of the moral law, men being censured for ignorance of that kind."[4] Nevertheless it must be admitted that invincible ignorance with regard to the moral law may exist. Even in an otherwise cultured environment much so-called moral illiteracy may be encountered. However, there are limits in this respect: the basic dictates of the moral order shine forth with a light so clear that no man possessing his senses can claim to be ignorant of them. When such ignorance is alleged, it is mostly done to cloak moral perversion.

Passions (emotions, affects) play an important part in human life. The affective side of our nature furnishes the driving forces in life. Out of emotions arise desires, urges, and motor impulses. Since the passions belong to the sense appetency they are directed toward objects of sense attraction and not toward the rational good. In themselves they contain no regulative principle and readily tend to excess. They are usually accompanied by a strong bodily resonance and produce a state of agitation and tension which seeks an outlet in external action. They arise unbidden in the presence of an appropriate object or at its mental representation. Thus the flood of angry sentiment that wells up in response to an insult and that, unless checked, immediately translates itself into outward actions. These tendencies can only be harmonized among themselves and subordinated to the moral good by the agency of reason and will, which by persistent discipline imposes on them right measure and directs them to the proper end.

In themselves passions are morally indifferent. Their moral quality is determined by the object which they embrace. They can be harnessed to a good or an evil purpose. If trained and controlled, they can be very helpful, but uncontrolled passions constitute a danger to the moral life and mental health. On account of their dynamic character they require strict supervision. They may lead to noble deeds or

[4] *Op. cit.*, III, 2.

to shameful criminal excesses. Whilst excellent servants, they are tyrannical and bad masters.

An aroused passion has the tendency to disorganize the whole mental life; as a consequence, it impairs critical reflection, beclouds judgment, overrides inhibitions, prevents deliberation, anticipates rational volition and causes impulsive action. Diminishing clear insight and in a large measure supplanting the will, it decreases voluntariness and responsibility. Unless, however, the suddenness and intensity of the passional upsurge are such that the action of reason is temporarily suspended, passion does not completely cancel accountability and the agent must answer for what is done under the influence of even a very violent passion.

The normal adult must have acquired self-mastery and control over his passions; if not, he is held responsible for the harmful actions to which they lead. Uncontrollable passion or irresistible impulse cannot be pleaded in justification of a crime because man should not be the puppet of his passions. It is the task of education and self-training to bring the passions under control. Passions (temper, anger, sensuality) which through the negligence or indulgence of parents get an unfair start may wreck a life.

The first movements of passion are not under rational control but spontaneously spring into being without any participation of the will. These strivings of passion and sensual desire may be disquieting but are in no sense sinful; they become culpable only when the mind fully adverts, and the will deliberately consents to them. Annoyingly, they may persist even after they have been vigorously repudiated. To understand this properly will save much anxiety.

Passion, especially sensuality, may be purposely evoked and fomented, and in that case, of course, is voluntary and severely blamable. This comes to pass by reading salacious literature, contemplating lewd pictures, assisting at obscene theatrical performances, seeking the occasion of sin, and voluptuous daydreaming.

Ethics does not demand the stoical suppression of the passions, but that they be kept within reasonable bounds and directed to worthy ends. Every passion needs discipline; only if duly disciplined can its inherent energy be turned into uesful channels and sublimated. Thus anger can be converted into moral indignation which will help to free the world from injustice and oppression. Significantly Holy Writ says :"Be angry, and sin not" (Eph. 4:26). There is a righteous anger, and this anger we might profitably turn against our own shortcomings. Blinding onrushes of passion, in legal parlance known as brainstorms, do not occur unless self-discipline has been woefully neglected. Without personal fault passions will rarely be able to grow to dangerous proportions. A passion does not result in violent and destructive outbursts if it has not been encouraged by the will and allowed to go unchecked for a long time.

Fear is a particularly upsetting passion which very frequently influences human conduct. It is the shrinking of the sense appetite from a threatening evil, especially from pain. Though not completely destroying, it lessens the voluntary character of an act. What is done from fear is done with reluctance yet is truly willed, except when the fear temporarily ousts reason, as may happen in the case of a panic. Fear may invalidate a contract (marriage) or render it rescindable. A common variety of fear is human respect which prevents many from acting according to their convictions. The trouble is that men dread many things (the scornful laughter of the impious, the sarcasm of the frivolous), which are not real evils at all, and, thus become moral cowards. We should cultivate a wholesome independence of the spirit with regard to the opinions of our fellow men and learn to fear only that which is evil in an absolute sense as the Lord says: "Be not afraid of them who kill the body and after that have no more that they can do" (Luke 12:4).

Violence excludes all voluntariness. It can only reach the external act but never touch the will itself. Only the body can be imprisoned, man's soul remains free even if he be in chains.

Both fatigue and disease lower vitality and psychic energy and so weaken the power of resistance to external influences. After long hours of monotonous toil the mind becomes particularly susceptible to the attractions of coarse sense pleasure.

No criminal trait can be directly inherited but a physical constitution which offers a favorable soil for the development of criminal tendencies may be transmitted. Birth does not doom anyone to crime. There is no psychic predestination. Nor are there any physical defects which directly produce a positive tendency to crime. A physical disability or deformity may, however, become an occasion of an antisocial disposition but this only through mental conditions to which it gives rise. Not of itself, but if coupled with native laziness, a physical handicap may lead to a career of petty thievery; in another individual the same deficiency may prove a spur to noteworthy achievement. The attitude of the social environment is very influential in determining on which of these courses the physically afflicted will enter. Whilst it may be confidently stated that there exists no definite physical criminal type, such as Lombroso and others have tried to make out, it cannot be denied that there is a favorable and an unfavorable heredity, to mention only emotional instability and untractable temperament. It is true that such disadvantages can be overcome but only by special effort, untiring perseverance, and rigorous discipline. Bad heredity will precipitate many a severe moral struggle which the more fortunate are spared.

3. HABIT AND VOLUNTARINESS

The influence of habits in life can scarcely be overrated. They are most intimately bound up with our weal or woe. As we grow, gradually larger and larger sections of our conduct are surrendered to habit which supersedes deliberation

and conscious effort, the original plasticity and indetermina-
tion of our native tendencies disappear, our actions fall into
definite grooves and a certain fixity settles on our whole life.
After a few years man is truly a bundle of habits. What this
means for good or bad can readily be understood. How
tenacious a habit can become may be gauged from the annoying persistence with which a little mannerism inadvert-
ently acquired clings to us. Not without good reason have
ingrained habits been called second nature.

A habit is an enduring quality, resulting from repeated
acts and disposing the agent to act in a particular manner.
Only faculties that are not determined to one mode of operation are susceptible of habits; faculties of this kind are the
rational faculties and the sense appetites and motor organs
which come under the control of the will. The habit produces a proneness toward an action, which, as a consequence,
is performed without effort, easily, well, and with pleasure.
Habits have their origin in acts, and as we are responsible
for our acts so are we responsible for the habits which grow
out of them. Since every act leaves a trace and begins or reinforces a habit, we must be ever on the alert lest some evil
or harmful habit take hold of us. Every deed is registered
in the mind and the nervous system and smooths the path
for the next deed. Continually we are spinning our own
fates.

The value of good habits is thus apparent. Without them
man would be like a reed shaken by every chance wind and
at the mercy of every impulse. Habits give stability, consistency, and uniformity to conduct and free man from the
tyranny of desire and caprice. Good resolutions are futile
unless they harden into habits. Grafted on our natural dispositions, habits form character and character determines the
general direction of our lives.

If a good habit is a valuable ally, a bad habit is a treacherous enemy. Evil habits acquired by self-indulgence in
youth remain with us to scourge us as the years roll on, to

destroy peace of mind, to bring about failure and to cause untold misery. Such habits become chains of slavery and barriers to success. Many a man groans under the chains which he has forged for himself, and drags them to his grave. This slavery is the more ignominious because it is self-induced and bred into bone and blood, into nerve and sinew. It is a bondage broken only with the utmost determination. W. James aptly speaks of the earthly hell which those prepare for themselves who habitually mold their characters in the wrong way. The thought should give pause to fond parents who in misunderstood love fasten on their children fetters that throughout life will be felt as a burden and produce much mental anguish.

By way of consolation and encouragement it should be stated that though it may be difficult to uproot a habit, no habit, however inveterate, is to be regarded as unconquerable wherever there is an honest will to overcome it.

What is done from force of habit, though in each single instance no longer fully deliberate, is indirectly voluntary as long as the habit is freely accepted and no effectual means are adopted for its extirpation. If, on the other hand, reform has honestly begun, the habit is sincerely regretted and disowned and constant and restraining watchfulness is exercised, the mechanical outcroppings of the habit are no longer imputable. Thus one who is bent on freeing himself from the ugly habit of profane speech will, for a time, unconsciously lapse into profane utterances until the reformation has been happily completed and the pertinent motor mechanism re-educated.

Good habits must not be permitted to become mechanical or automatic (as might happen in the case of oral prayer) for thus the merit of the individual act would be lessened or even completely nullified. To prevent the deterioration of good habits, they should, at reasonable intervals, be revitalized and lifted again to the level of conscious and deliberate activity.

Mechanical habits which are the mere outcome of an enforced external routine and have not been inwardly accepted are neither lasting nor of any great moral value. This explains the moral collapse in later life of so many who have passed through a prolonged course of what on the surface seems excellent institutional training. Practices that have not taken hold on the inner man are quickly shed when the external pressure necessitating compliance is removed. Moral habits are not acquired passively but demand wholehearted internal response and cooperation.

4. ENVIRONMENT AND MORAL CHARACTER

The formative influences emanating from the social surroundings in which man lives are known as informal training. Whilst imponderable and intangible, their action is very pronounced and resembles that of the all-pervasive atmosphere. All bear the imprint of their social environment, which colors their ideals, affects their moral appreciations and forms their standards of conduct. Distorted moral judgments and moral insensibility frequently have their origin in unfavorable environmental conditions. The reason for the influence of environment is to be sought in the social nature of man and his imitative tendencies. Of course, environment is not omnipotent, many triumph over it; still a bad environment usually leaves character sadly scarred. Hence, if we wish to judge a transgression with justice we must take into account the social antecedents of the transgressor.

The corporate life that flows around us influences us not so much through an explicit code of precepts or a definite set of injunctions as through its prevailing tone and spirit. It exerts a continual pressure either of a degrading or uplifting nature. The family circle and the neighborhood constitute the first contacts of the child with the social environment and are the most decisive factors in moral development.

Whatever may be the part of environment in the formation of character, man withal is a creature of his own making. Accordingly, environment will not absolve a man of responsibility for his actions.

V

The Moral Act

1. INTERNAL AND EXTERNAL ACTS

Will is the power of choice which exercises control over the other faculties of man. It is the pivot on which all moral conduct turns, for from it go forth the fiats and commands executed by the various powers of mind and body. Of the acts of the internal will, moral qualities are primarily and formally predicated, whereas the acts of the other faculties derive their morality from their dependence on the will. Ordinarily, the will act expresses itself in corresponding external deeds and the inward and outward act are conjoined as body and soul constituting a unit, but the decision of the will is the crucial element. Should the execution of the evil purpose be impeded, the will nevertheless contracts its malice. A man may be a thief at heart though the actual theft cannot be carried out from want of opportunity. The willful desire defiles the soul. By the same token the good deed is credited even if untoward circumstances thwart the sincere intention of the agent. Within limits we take the will for the deed. Success is not in our power. In this sense we accept Kant's dictum: "A good will is good not because of what it performs or effects, but simply by virtue of the volition. Even if it should happen that, owing to special disfavor of fortune, or the niggardly provision of a stepmotherly nature, this will should wholly lack power to accomplish its purpose, if with its greatest effort it should yet achieve nothing, and there should only remain the good will (not to be sure, a mere wish, but the summoning of all means in our power), then, like a jewel, it would still shine by its own luster, as a thing which has its whole value in itself."[1]

An intention, however, that always stops short of external accomplishment cannot be taken as evidence of a serious will and is devoid of merit.

2. INDIRECT RESPONSIBILITY

Our actions frequently are linked to effects or consequences from which they cannot be dissociated. These in most cases can be foreseen and may not be ignored. They entail indirect responsibility from which the agent cannot escape. The reckless driver cannot repudiate responsibility for the harm which he causes on the plea that it was not intended because, though not willed in itself, it was willed in the action from which it followed. He who picks up one link of a chain draws the others after it. The mind cannot arbitrarily separate what is connected in the order of causal relationship. The outcome of an action belongs to the action. If the effect must be avoided, the cause likewise must be avoided. Thoughtlessness and indifference in this respect involve guilt proportionate to the seriousness of the results emanating from the directly willed act. Habitual unconcern for the injury which our conduct may inflict on others bespeaks moral callousness and ingrained selfishness. Indirect responsibility extends farther than most like to think. Too many shut their eyes to the evil which follows in the wake of their actions.

There are, however, occasions when an evil effect may be permitted provided it is not directly intended and there is a compensatory good effect which follows with equal immediacy as the evil one. The evil effect in this case is not the actual means to procure the good in question, for to do evil in order that good may ensue is always wrong. The principle

[1] *Op. cit.,* I.

invoked in this situation, where a very desirable good cannot be obtained without a simultaneously occurring evil result, is known as the principle of the double effect. It affords a rule of action for difficult cases and must always be used with great caution. Its practical application calls both for considerable casuistical skill and the greatest moral sincerity.

3. THE DETERMINANTS OF MORALITY

By these we understand the various factors which give to the individual act its moral entity and invest it with specific qualities of goodness or badness. They are the objects toward which the act is directed in virtue of its own inherent tendency, the circumstances that surround the act or the concrete setting in which it happens, and the end which inspires, prompts or instigates the act. Any one of these factors may vitiate the act and render it morally evil.

The object here is taken in the moral sense. Thus the object of theft is not just money physically considered but money belonging to another. Under this moral aspect the object is the internal constituent of the act and accordingly determines its nature and character. It is the innermost core of the action and imparts to the deed its content and meaning. Deeds carry with them something which makes them right or wrong in themselves. We can determine our own aims and purposes but we cannot change the essential nature of acts. There is an objective moral order which the will must accept; there are deeds which the will cannot make good. Certain deeds have values of their own independently of any estimation of man. It is not true to say: "There is nothing right or wrong, but thinking makes it so." If this were so, morality would be hopelessly vague and arbitrary; it would become a matter of caprice. Accordingly, in this connection it is untrue what Kant says: "Nothing can possibly be conceived in the world which can be called good without qualification except a good will." The will derives its goodness not from its own intentions but from its conformity with the right order of things.

The object specifies the act, stamps it with a definite character, puts it in its proper class and gives it a distinctive name as theft, murder, lying. Hence the deed derives its essential, intrinsic, and specific goodness or badness from the object toward which it tends and which it embraces. This internal complexion of the deed cannot be altered by an external supervening factor. If the object is bad, the act is irremediably bad and remains so.

Circumstances affect the morality of the act; they impart an intrinsic but accidental goodness or badness because they also enter into the internal constitution of the act by modifying the object. Objects actually do appear in a concrete setting and acts are performed under certain definite attending conditions of time, place, and manner, from which they cannot be isolated; consequently, these circumstances, which may be of great importance, must be taken into consideration when the moral quality of the act is to be determined. The thief does not just steal but he steals much or little, he steals from a rich or poor person, and these circumstances may make a considerable difference in the evaluation of the deed. There are aggravating and extenuating circumstances.

4. ENDS, INTENTIONS, MOTIVES

Though not identical in meaning, the three terms are so closely allied that for all practical purposes they may be used interchangeably. They refer to that which arouses volition.

The morality of the deed is unalterably fixed by the object whereas the moral character of the doer is determined by the ends, intentions, and motives which habitually prompt his conduct. These furnish a clue to his moral attitude and give evidence of the basic tendencies of his personality. The end is the ultimate spring of human activity for the end is that which is regarded as good and on account of which an act is done. Now what appears good or desirable to a man is indicative of his whole moral outlook and his habitual preferences. The end is closest to the heart of man and everything is done for its sake and subordinated to its attainment. It enters more deeply into subjective morality than any other element. He who habitually sets himself unselfish ends and acts from unselfish motives is unselfish, and he whose actions are mostly inspired by selfish motives is selfish. A sordid end, all agree, spoils the best deed and robs it of its beauty.

The execution of a purpose, however, always requires means and these likewise enter into volition; in fact they are more immediately willed than the end and thus contribute to the complex act of intention and execution a quality of their own. If they are immoral the whole complex is vitiated for the end in view has no power to change the nature of the means employed, since as we have previously seen the intrinsic goodness or badness of an act depends on the thing willed or the object of volition. The end does not enter into the internal constitution of the act but is the efficient cause of its existence. It belongs to the doer not to the deed. The intention, therefore, is not everything, the nature of the deed must be considered. To make the end or intention the determining element in morality would lead to moral subjectivism, because, in that case, since the end depends on our choice we could make any action good, all objective criteria of morality would vanish and everybody could create his own moral values. The object cannot be manipulated by the will but must be taken as it is. Its meaning and value are fixed by an objective ontological order which our subjective attitude is unable to change. To attribute moral value exclusively to the intention or the motive spells the end of all objective morality and lands us in pure utilitarianism. Nothing is more subversive of all morality than the proposition that a good end can sanction the use of evil means, that one may lie or steal, provided that the motive is laudable. It is precisely to this plea that evildoers readily resort in self-justification. Criminals can always assign good motives in defense of their actions.

Alleged motives must be suspected if they do not find verification in appropriate conduct. The conflict between motives and deeds lays one open to the charge of moral dishonesty and insincerity. We are rather biased in interpreting our own motives and read them to favor our egotism. Overt acts in this respect are more eloquent than professed hidden sentiments. The man who feels it necessary to excuse or justify his deeds by an appeal to his good intentions mostly mistakes his real motives. He is not quite as good and unselfish and noble in his sentiments as he would try to make himself and others believe. There is a flaw in his character and he is a victim of self-deception. If he sounded his motives honestly, he would discover that they are tainted. Whoever has need of vindicating himself by an appeal to the purity and disinterestedness of his motives should be mistrusted and should not trust himself. There is most likely much pharisaism in his moral make-up. Thus the strict disciplinarian, who exacts punctilious observance of minor rules and has no appreciation of the discomfort which his harsh insistence on the carrying out of his minutest orders causes, flatters himself that he is animated by a high regard for duty, when in reality his treatment of his inferiors is motivated by gross selfishness and lack of self-discipline. A virtue and a devotion to duty which uniformly bring suffering and inconvenience to others are not genuine.

Whilst we cannot admit that a good intention alone will stamp an action as good, we readily grant that the well-intentioned man ordinarily will act in conformity with the moral law. We may go farther and say that a man who habitually pursues noble aims and cultivates high ideals will mostly be right in his moral judgments and not easily be tempted to employ dubious means. He will be quick to detect the incongruous character of the means and reject it without hesitation. This, however, is true only when the motive is really pure and has no fatal admixture of selfishness in it. In this sense the Gospel says: "If thy eye be single, thy whole body shall be lightsome" (Matt. 6:22). Still a mistaken judgment is possible so that a man, in the interests of what he deems a good cause, will adopt objectionable methods. Therefore it is necessary explicitly to condemn the seductive principle that the end sanctifies the means. However noble the end may be, it cannot justify an evil act, because, being extraneous to the act, it cannot change its reprehensible character. The public weal cannot be promoted by oppression of the people or injustice of any kind. The glamour of the end may blind an individual to the perverseness of the means by which the pretended good is achieved. Statesmen may easily fall into this subtle snare and condone immoral policies on the plea that they are conducive to the common good. Such a course bears evil fruits. Father Gaston Sortais, S.J., in his *Traité de Philosophie,* exclaims: "What dastardly crimes have been proposed or committed in the name of the welfare of the state." Medicine, like statecraft, may be snared by the same pitfall for it also is concerned with a good by which men set great store such as life, health, and physical well-being and is frequently brought face to face with critical situations. The physician and surgeon, therefore, also must be warned of the fallacious character of the principle in question. Even to save a life or to ensure racial betterment evil may not be done. Thus euthanasia, eugenical sterilization, contraception, direct abortion, craniotomy stand condemned. What is contrary to the moral law can never be justified by medical science. The moral law is supreme and absolute. Against all sophisms arising from false pity and misguided sympathy, Pius XI, in the encyclical *On Christian Marriage,* proclaims the inviolability of God's law: "No reason, however grave, may be put forward by which anything intrinsically against nature may become conformable to nature and morally good."

To indorse the principle that a good intention can blot out the inherent wickedness of an act would upset the entire moral order and create a loophole for the introduction of every evil practice.

It is true, however, that a lofty purpose adorns a good act with an added grace or imparts moral beauty to an otherwise indifferent act. The good end enriches moral acts and gives them a fuller moral coloring. We might say that it embroiders a beautiful design on a fine material. This additional goodness is of an external and accidental character. Almsgiving, in itself an act of charity, may in its end take on the additional goodness of an act of penance and of religion. A journey undertaken to commit a sin is a wicked journey. A visit to the sick is an errand of mercy. So the trivial actions of everyday life can be transfigured into things of beauty as George Herbert observes in *The Elixir:*

> A servant with this clause
> Makes drudgery divine;
> Who sweeps a room as for thy laws
> Makes that and th' action fine.

VI

Pleasure and Pain

1. PLEASURE AND MORALITY

Pleasure holds such a large place in human consciousness and is so highly valued and spontaneously sought by men that no theory of conduct can possibly ignore it but must fit it into the context of life and positively correlate it with moral ends. Most of our experiences are pervaded by an affective tone and accompanied by agreeable feeling, whence the question arises to what extent, if at all, the attendant pleasantness may motivate the choice of an action. May our conduct be determined by no other thought than to enjoy pleasure and to escape pain?

Whilst in the animal kingdom pleasure and pain may be the sovereign masters, in the life of a rational being they cannot be accorded this commanding position. Reason recognizes pleasure as a good of a lower order that must be duly subordinated to values of a higher kind. Pleasure is incidental and its function is to secure actions that have an ulterior purpose. It serves as an incentive to otherwise useful activities but is not itself the purpose of activity. Our sentient appetites impel us to seek primarily the objects conducive to our well-being and only secondarily the gratification annexed to them. In the economy of nature it is so arranged that the proper use of a faculty yields delight in order to compensate for the effort required in the performance of the act and to lead to its repetition.

2. PLEASURE AS AN END

There exists a practical agreement among men that a life dedicated exclusively to the pursuit of pleasure is a life lived on a subhuman level. Pleasure is essentially selfish and it is impossible to see anything noble and commanding respect in pure self-seeking. If made the chief goal of life, pleasure has a degrading and vulgarizing effect and proves an obstacle to worthy achievement and spiritual growth. The lure of pleasure is a snare which effectually prevents upward striving and lulls to sleep all higher aspirations. It does not spur us on to progress but eventuates in stagnation. A Chinese proverb says: "To fail, do what you like; to succeed, like what you do."

Whereas normally man acts with pleasure, he does not directly act for pleasure. It bespeaks an unwholesome condition of mind when a man is actuated directly by the desire for pleasure, since pleasure is not for its own sake but for the activity to which it is attached. It should be borne in mind that pleasure seeking, when erected into an end, defeats itself, and is of all pursuits the most disappointing in which a man can engage. The futility of living merely for enjoyment cannot be too strongly impressed upon the young. In that direction lies frustration. It is the bitter experience of the pleasure seeker that the pleasures so ardently coveted, when attained, turn out to be Dead Sea fruit and so his life very often is the most unhappy of lives. The surest way to get pleasure is to forget it. Pleasures which come unbidden and unsought in the performance of the ordinary tasks of life outweigh anything for which the thrill hunter feverishly strives. Pleasure adds an agreeable flavor and fragrance to life but it is not a thing to be lived for. A life spent for pleasure is a wasted life.

But acting for pleasure and living for pleasure are not the same. Whilst the latter constitutes a manifest misuse of life, the former may be perfectly lawful. Accordingly, an action

which in itself is not immoral and conforms to the circumstances of one's state of life, may be done on account of its
pleasureableness. This excludes all extramarital sex gratification. Since God has attached pleasure to certain physical
operations, to intend that pleasure cannot be wrong in itself
because it does not disturb the objective order. Of course, an
element of disorder may be introduced by excess. One may
prefer a tasty dish to a less palatable one even though the
latter be equally nutritious. As long as the end of the act is
not definitely excluded, the subordination of pleasure to
the purposes of the natural order and the plan of the Creator
is implicitly accepted. The situation changes entirely when
the pleasure is detached from the end which it is intended to
procure and the natural outcome of the act frustrated for
such a course thwarts the designs of nature, interferes with
the right order and, consequently, indicates a perverse will.

3. THE VIRTUE OF TEMPERANCE

To regulate the enjoyment of pleasure, which, if left to
itself, would easily tend to excess, belongs to the virtue of
temperance. It operates chiefly in the realm of sense appetency for there the attraction of pleasure is particularly
strong and the danger of excess and disorder ever present.
Its aim is to keep within reasonable bounds the satisfaction
of bodily wants and to bring them into harmony with life's
highest end. It is opposed to gluttony (the immoderate indulgence in food and drink) and lust (the selfish misuse of
the procreative faculty). Its most common forms are abstinence, soberness, and chastity but it stands for moderation in all things. The high esteem in which it was held even
by the pagans is due to the fact that it promotes physical
health, fosters mental development, increases general efficiency and makes for undisturbed serenity of life. In business and industry temperance is greatly appreciated.

Temperance extends also to the outward manifestations
of the emotions such as anger, joy, hilarity, the expressions

of which ought to be characterized by becoming restraint.
The whole external comportment of man must give evidence
of self-possession and dignity. Under this aspect, temperance
is known as modesty, lack of which renders our conduct
offensive to others and indicates poor breeding. Human
nature in the raw is a very unpleasing sight and a source of
great annoyance. Unrestrained boisterousness, an unneces-
sarily elevated voice and loud laughter jar and irritate those
around us.

Temperance can only be acquired by practicing self-denial
and exercising severity toward ourselves. Continual yielding
to the attraction of sense pleasure shatters all self-control and
reduces the will to impotence. Professor W. James advises
men to do something occasionally for no other reason than
that they would rather not do it and likens such effort to the
insurance a man pays against evil days. It stores up moral
reserves on which one may draw when the allurements of
pleasure become particularly insistent. He who has not
learned to refuse his senses what they may demand will
sooner or later give in to their unrestrained cravings and
find himself enslaved by the blandishments of sensuality.
Self-abnegation, thus, is essential for the maintenance of the
supremacy of the will and proves itself to be a postulate of
natural reason. A favorite maxim of the old philosophers
was: *Sustine et abstine,* "Bear and refrain."

He who would acquire the virtue of temperance and remain master of himself must above all keep the imagination
under control, for it is this disturbing faculty which in-
flames the sense appetite and, by continually inventing new
objects of gratification, breeds insatiable desires. The natural
desires quickly come to rest but the artificially stimulated desires know no limits. Discipline of the imagination is a
prime factor in moral as well as mental hygiene.

Practices which aid in the acquisition of self-control are
called ascetical and correspond to the training which an
athlete undergoes to fit himself for arduous feats of physical

prowess. We may, then, say that asceticism is not a gloomy renunciation of all sense satisfaction or a despairing flight from pleasure but a means of self-discipline enabling us to emancipate ourselves from the tyranny of desire and impulse and to use pleasure in conformity with the dictates of reason. It does not make us spurn all pleasures but secures for us a sovereign independence, which prevents us from being enslaved by them. In fact contempt for pleasure, e.g., aesthetical enjoyment, may be entirely devoid of moral significance. Unless really growing out of a spiritualized character, it may indicate nothing more than a sullen and morose disposition, a lack of aesthetic sentiment or an unsocial nature. Pleasure should neither be despised nor overprized. It is quite in keeping with man's nature to seek pleasure as an incentive to appropriate activity. But in all cases moderation must be observed and excess avoided. In this respect no man can be safe unless he cultivates an ascetical attitude and a prudent reserve. As soon as one discovers that the thought of pleasure begins to haunt the mind and produce a state of restlessness, it becomes necessary to exercise a stricter self-control. The moment pleasure interferes with the plain course of duty it must be dropped. Only on such conditions is it possible to attain to that freedom and detachment which enable a man to inhibit unlawful sensual movements before they become deliberate and enter on the stage of external motor action. The habit of looking for pleasure or the hedonistic mood breaks down all safeguards and leaves a man helpless in the presence of the enticements of illicit sense gratification. The almost complete abandonment of ascetical traditions in our times has reduced the present generation to this sorry plight.

The qualitative difference between pleasures must not be ignored. Sensual pleasure appeals to the animal side of man, intellectual enjoyment to his spiritual nature. The latter is of a more ennobling, lasting, and satisfying character. It should be preferred and a taste for it cultivated, for as St.

Augustine in his *Confessions* says: "It makes a difference from what source a man draws his enjoyment."

4. AMUSEMENTS AND RECREATION

By amusements we understand pleasant occupations of all sorts, both mental and physical, by which attention is diverted from the serious pursuits of life and from which an agreeable state of relaxation results. Occasional relief from the stress and strain of work is needed if body and mind are not to be overtaxed. Inasmuch as amusements really refresh the mind and help the body to recuperate its exhausted resources they are morally justified. Under the category of amusements come play of every kind, games, sports, dances, banquets, pleasure cruises, stage performances, screen productions, frolics, social gatherings, music, the contemplation of objects of art and light reading. The choice of the right kind of amusements is of great importance for character development and even bodily health.

Besides having great restorative power, amusements possess positive social value when they promote good fellowship, encourage the spirit of teamwork and fair play, and offer opportunities for the practice of charity, self-control, kindness, and subordination. In this case they help in the upbuilding of desirable personality traits and in the acquisition of graceful habits. Aversion to social amusements may be a sign of morbid antisocial tendencies. Games are useful in overcoming introversion. Play both reveals and forms character.

Amusements, however harmless in themselves, are rendered objectionable by untimeliness and excess. When they merely serve to kill time which ought to be employed for self-improvement, or to make one oblivious of the higher aims of life they cease to be good. Such amusements carried to inordinate lengths frequently fill the emptiness of a life which is self-centered and devoid of nobler interests. Indulgence in amusements which degenerates into dissipation and entails a waste of money and physical and mental resources merits condemnation. If amusements create a distaste for higher pursuits, as fondness for novel reading might produce a dislike for serious literature, they are no longer commendable. In all cases, the attraction of pleasure constitutes an insidious temptation which calls for constant vigilance.

With many amusements evil is directly associated because they inordinately arouse the lower appetites. Unwholesome amusements of this type must be sedulously shunned. Commercialized amusement too often is of this debasing character. Dr. A. F. Findley formulates a rule that will serve well in the selection of amusements: "From the individual's point of view, it is important that he should learn to avoid every form of pleasure which is physically harmful or morally degrading, and to allow himself only that measure of enjoyment which is consistent with the proper discharge of his work, and with a due concern for higher personal interests, such as self-culture and religious worship. Indulgence in pleasure even the most innocent is illegitimate when it leads to the neglect of our social obligations."[1]

5. SOCIETY AND POPULAR AMUSEMENTS

Society has very much at stake in this matter. Nowhere are the contacts between the respectable and the criminal classes more frequent and more intimate than in places of public entertainment, and right here is the point where many an inexperienced youth is drawn into the vortex of the underworld. The first steps in crime are very often linked to dangerous forms of recreation. It is in the best interests of society to supply the people with ample opportunities for wholesome enjoyment.

Proper recreation is necessary as a preventive of juvenile delinquency. With some exaggeration but with a goodly measure of truth Miss Jane Addams claims "that recreation is stronger than vice and that recreation alone can stifle the

[1] *Encyclopedia of Religion and Ethics,* under "Amusements."

lust for vice."[2] Statistics show that wherever supervised playgrounds are maintained in crowded neighborhoods a marked
decrease in juvenile delinquency may be observed. Recreation can serve as an apprenticeship in antisocial behavior
but it can also become a training school for social conduct.
Hence the responsibility of society in this respect is obvious.

The general moral tone pervading the social atmosphere
depends very much on the prevailing forms of popular
recreation. To foster ennobling forms of social pleasure and
to suppress undesirable ones is a very effective means of im-
proving public morals. The commercialized amusements, if
they are not to become a threat to civilization, must be entrusted to men of moral integrity and strictly supervised.
This is rarely done and too often, as Miss Addams says, "the
Anglo-Saxon city has turned over the provision for public
recreation to the most evilminded and most unscrupulous
members of the community."[3] The desire for profit has led
these purveyors of pleasure to cater to the vilest tastes and
the lowest instincts.

Society should provide pleasures which are truly recrea-
tive. Unfortunately that is not true of many of our popular
amusements of which Dr. Charles A. Ellwood pens this severe indictment: "Our world presents the amazing spectacle
of more lives offered upon the altars of pleasure than upon
those of war, famine, and pestilence combined. The lives
utterly ruined, or their social usefulness at least destroyed,
by the pursuit of foolish pleasures are so numerous that no
attempt is made to keep track of them."[4]

Social pleasure should also be educational and assist in
building up the right sort of social character in individuals.
This educational and socializing effect of pleasure need not
in the least detract from its recreational value. Moreover,
social pleasures can be spiritualized so that they will call into

---

[2] *The Spirit of Youth and the City Streets*, p. 20.
[3] *Ibid.*, p. 7.
[4] Ellwood, C. A., *The Reconstruction of Religion*, Macmillan Co., N. Y.,
p. 269.

play man's higher faculties. The element of art may be in fused into them, which would remove many of the objectionable features now so conspicuous. Tersely the encyclical *Vigilanti Cura* of Pius XI sums up the whole problem in the following passage: "Recreation in its manifold varieties has become a necessity for people who labor under the fatiguing conditions of modern industry. But it must be worthy of the rational nature of man, and therefore must be morally healthy. It must be elevated to the rank of a positive factor for good, and must seek to arouse noble sentiments."

But on the whole, no signal improvement in the quality of social pleasure will be effected until a greater measure of moral discipline in individuals is restored.

6.   PAIN   AND   SUFFERING

Our terrestrial abode is, in the language of John Keats, a "vale of soul making," and in this process pain, suffering, sorrow, loss, bereavement, and hardships have an important function. Precisely as it is, this world presents itself as a fit medium for the development of character. Not those who are cradled in luxury and ease attain to the fullest personal development but rather those who have passed through the shadows and have been purified in fiery furnaces.

Experience warrants the assertion that an economy of unalloyed pleasure would be disastrous to man; the elimination of pain would condemn the race to stagnation and degeneration. A life into which suffering in some form or other does not enter will invariably be a life devoid of achievement and heroic grandeur. Pain is necessary to bring out the good and to plough up the soul in order to prepare a fertile soil for virtue. The cult of pain is unreasonable but a recognition of the useful function of pain in human experience conforms to reason. A whole catalogue of beautiful virtues — patience, sympathy, courage, resourcefulness, loyalty, hope, self-sacrifice — would drop out of existence if there were no suffering to endure and no obstacles to overcome. The complete coincidence of goodness with happiness is not in this world. Every day brings home to us the lesson that the best lives are not immune from suffering and sorrow. The highest human life cannot be reached except through the death of that which is low and sordid. In this sense Tennyson writes in *In Memoriam:*

> I held it true, with him who sings
> To one clear harp in diverse tones,
> That men may rise on stepping-stones
> Of their dead selves to higher things.

Pain is the result of the struggle between the higher and the lower and prepares the victory for that which is best. When a guilty man is tortured by remorse, it means that the better self has been quickened, and that the true good is asserting itself against the lie which has held him captive and is shattering the illusion in which his soul has been wrapped. Pain opens the eyes of those engaged in wrongdoing and reveals to them the innermost tendency of evil. It is punitive and retributory, but chiefly disciplinary and educative. Were there no suffering, no regret, no shame, no disgrace to follow as a shadow on wrongdoing, moral evil would enjoy a sort of unchallenged and authorized existence. Sin would seem to have an undisputed right in the scheme of things if it did not recoil on the perpetrator or bring misery to his victims. How often is a transgressor brought to the perception of the wickedness of his ways by the spectacle of the sufferings which his deeds have caused to others! Thus the suffering of the innocent becomes a great redemptive force. The presence of pain indicates that man is recoverable, that ameliorative forces are at work around him and within him. His own experiences and those of his fellow men hold up the mirror in which are reflected the miseries following from a lustful will, the calamities lurking in immorality, the generations poisoned by vice. Pain clarifies the vision of the individual and the race to behold the effects of wrongdoing.

It proves, as a consequence, a tremendous energy for moralizing man and society. It vindicates the moral government of the world and limits the reign of moral evil which, without this ever present protest, would hold unimpeded and approved sway. Yes, moral evil is in this world, but says Dr. Andrew Martin Fairbanks: "It continues to exist not as a rightful or permanent inhabitant of the universe, but as one whose very right to be is denied, and for whose expulsion all the energies of nature have been marshalled and trained to fight."[5]

Suffering, however, is not only a regenerative but also a propulsive force. It has done more for human progress than its opposite pleasure which tempts man to rest in comfortable ease.

Not enjoyment is the purpose of this life, but growth. But for growth both sunshine and rain are necessary. Pain chastens and, for the development of the spiritual self, is more important than pleasure. Men are formed in the school of sorrow and hardship and defeat. To be spared misfortunes in this life is the greatest misfortune that could befall one. If we could penetrate beneath the surface we would come to the conclusion that our pains and sorrows actually have been our greatest opportunities. It may also be added that loss and suffering do not necessarily bring unhappiness. Frequently they throw us back on our deeper selves and lead us to the discovery of newer and purer sources of joy. As Shakespeare states in *As You Like It,* "Sweet are the uses of adversity."

[5] *The Philosophy of the Christian Religion,* p. 167.

VII

Hedonism and Utilitarianism

1. PLEASURE THE CRITERION OF MORALITY

Hedonistic ethics (the ethics of pleasure) appear in the crude form of egotistic hedonism, which affirms that the individual's own interests are in every case the dominant good, and in the more refined form of utilitarianism (universalistic hedonism, sympathetic utilitarianism), which makes the greatest happiness of the greatest number the essential criterion of morality. Common to both is the interpretation of the good in terms of pleasurable experience. Both also agree in this that the consequences of the act constitute its goodness or badness. The fundamental flaw of the ethics of pleasure is that it centers its attention exclusively on this world and lets the next world take care of itself. It considers man merely as a child of time and a sentient being. Hedonism in ethics is the natural outcome of sensationalism in psychology. If the self is nothing more than the sum of his passing experiences, and there is no abiding selfhood, patently the momentary feelings assume supreme importance. Logically, a hedonistic ethics will be adopted by all who ignore the spiritual side of man and restrict his existence to this world. It is by its whole tenor a morality of the earth, earthy. It is saved from grossness only by the inconsistency with which it escapes the ugly consequences flowing from its fundamental tenets. Thus the unselfishness demanded by utilitarianism has no adequate support in the system itself, which can recognize no other basis of action save pure egotism. Nor can a qualitative difference between pleasures be maintained unless a principle of value other than that of mere agreeable feeling be introduced. Once the good is identified with pleasure, the greater good can only consist in a greater amount of pleasure. But if utilitarianism cannot uphold a qualitative difference between pleasures nor furnish a valid ground for altruism, but on the contrary must put all pleasures on the same level and reduce virtue to a hedonistic calculus and altruism to disguised selfishness, we understand that the sentiments of the normal man rebel against it. That was the reaction of his contemporaries to the utilitarian ethics of Jeremy Bentham, as Dr. Philip Wheelwright remarks: "Bentham's formulation of the theory had aroused vigorous hostility. To suppose that life had no nobler end than the pursuit of pleasure seemed to many persons a doctrine utterly mean and grovelling, worthy only of swine. Carlyle referred to the doctrine as a pig-philosophy."[1]

2. EXPOSITION OF THE THEORY

John Stuart Mill defines utilitarianism as follows: "The creed which accepts as the foundation of morals utility, or the Greatest Happiness Principle, holds that actions are right in proportion as they tend to promote happiness, wrong as they tend to produce the reverse of happiness. By happiness is intended pleasure and the absence of pain; by unhappiness, pain and the privation of pleasure."[2]

Bentham sets forth his views in these terms: "Nature has placed mankind under the guidance of two sovereign masters, pain and pleasure. It is for them alone to point out what we ought to do, as well as to determine what we shall do. . . . By the principle of utility is meant that principle which approves or disapproves of every action whatsoever, accord-

[1] Wheelwright, Dr. P., *A Critical Introduction to Ethics,* The Odyssey Press, N. Y., p. 83.
[2] *Utilitarianism,* p. 9.

ing to the tendency which it appears to have to augment or diminish the happiness of the party whose interest is in question. . . . Pleasure is in itself a good, and, the only good; pain is in itself an evil, the only evil."[3] Again in *Deontology:* "To prove that the immoral action is a miscalculation of self-interest, to show how erroneous an estimate the vicious man makes of pains and pleasures, is the purpose of the intelligent moralist."

3. EVALUATION OF UTILITARIANISM

Utilitarianism is unable to account for the imperative character of duty and to explain the respect which we have for virtue. If morality is nothing but a seeking of enjoyment and virtue nothing more than correct hedonistic arithmetic and a nice balancing of pleasures, a mere sense of humor should prevent us wasting fine language on the splendor of the moral law and the reverential obedience owed it by mankind. The utilitarian view contradicts the common sentiments of mankind according to which the practice of virtue is something quite distinct from the pursuit of pleasure and virtue itself essentially opposed to selfishness. In fact, the conscious endeavor to practice virtue merely as a means to happiness must prove barren. Genuine virtue will at times require a complete renunciation of happiness. This Mill himself admits: "These only are happy, I thought, who have their minds fixed on some object other than their own happiness; on the happiness of others, on the improvement of mankind, even on some art or pursuit, followed not as a means, but as an ideal end. Aiming thus at something else, they find happiness by the way."[4] Thereby Mill disproves his own theory and admits that the good, and not happiness, is the object of human striving.

In the common apprehension of mankind, disinterestedness is an essential element of virtuous conduct, which is

[3] *Introduction to the Principles of Morals and Legislation,* I.
[4] Mill, John Stuart, *Autobiography,* p. 142.

vitiated to the extent that calculating interest enters into its motivation. To forego pleasure with a view of receiving in return some other pleasure no more answers to our idea of virtue than to lend money at interest to our idea of charity. The idea of a profitable investment is alien to the concept of the virtue of charity.

As a practical criterion of judging the rightness or wrongness of an action the utilitarian principle of consequences likewise breaks down for the exact estimate of the pleasant or unpleasant consequences of various possible courses of action presents insurmountable difficulties. On account of the complicated nature of human actions and their far-reaching repercussions such forecasts would be very problematic and could serve no practical purpose.

Within the limits of utilitarianism no ground can be shown for distinguishing pleasures into higher or lower. But the distinction is commonly accepted. Men will feel deep humiliation at having to admit that they have derived pleasure from indulging in certain amusements which on reflection they recognize as incompatible with the nobility of human nature. When Mill discriminates between different kinds of pleasure on the score that, while some appeal to the more elevated faculties of man, others satisfy only his animal appetites, he evidently introduces a principle foreign to utilitarianism, namely, that of conformity to human nature. The sense of dignity which makes a man spurn lower pleasures, even if they are more intense, itself rises above the sphere of pleasure.

Utilitarianism withal is not a selfish doctrine. It stresses the essentially social nature of man and recognizes the sympathetic impulse in man as a natural endowment. It urges the individual to live not for himself but for the greatest happiness of the greatest number. It is democratic in its general tendency and aims at setting up a community in which all have equal rights and none enjoy special privileges to the disadvantage of the rest. Both Bentham and J. Stuart Mill were noted social reformers of their day and they framed their utilitarian ethics to serve as an effective instrument of social reform. The system may be used to render valuable service in this respect but it is liable also to fearful abuse. Its possibilities for abuse spring from the fact that it fails to give clear expression to the rights of the individual. The danger of abuse is increased by its confusion of the social and political with the ethical end of life, a confusion which has culminated in the Totalitarianism of our days. How easily utilitarianism can be distorted into an instrument of oppression in the sense of Totalitarianism and Communism appears from the following quotations. Alexander Bain writes: "Utility is opposed to the selfish principle, for, as propounded, it always implies the good of society generally and the subordination of individual interests to the general good."[5] And Mill: "The social state is at once so natural, so necessary, and so habitual to man, that except in some unusual circumstances or by an effort of voluntary abstraction, he never conceives of himself otherwise than as a member of a body."[6]

The altruism advocated by the utilitarianists accordingly must be hedged around with various safeguards. The individual cannot totally be referred either to others or the community. His relations to others do not make up the whole man. There remains something which belongs to him and his Creator. Man is at once a social and an individual being. To deny either is to mutilate him. Man's ethical end transcends his social end and must prevail if a conflict arises between the two. Utilitarian altruism has the fatal tendency of obscuring man's inner being and of ignoring that individual good which lies beyond society.

Mill is very anxious to free utilitarianism from the imputation of selfishness. He expects no small degree of self-sacrifice when he writes: "The utilitarian morality does recognize

[5] *Emotions and Will*, p. 308.
[6] Mill, John Stuart, *Autobiography*, p. 143.

in human beings the power of sacrificing their own greatest good for the good of others . . . I must again repeat what the assailants of utilitarianism have seldom the justice to acknowledge: that the happiness which forms the utilitarian standard of what is right in conduct is not the agent's own happiness but that of all concerned; as between himself and others utilitarianism requires him to be as strictly impartial as a disinterested and benevolent spectator."[7] The insistent question here is, can so lofty a superstructure of altruistic and self-sacrificing conduct be erected on the pleasure principle which is the heart of utilitarianism? Pleasure is essentially self-regarding. Man by nature pursues his own happiness but it would be absurd to maintain that he necessarily pursues the happiness of others. Benevolence and altruism cannot draw their inspiration from the pleasure principle. Hedonistic utilitarianism can demand unselfishness and self-sacrifice only at the cost of logical consistency.

The evolutionary utilitarianism of Herbert Spencer adds a new touch inasmuch as it holds that the forces of natural evolution are constantly working toward a more perfect adaptation of egotistic to altruistic interests so that eventually they will coincide. When this stage has been reached the sense of moral obligation will vanish. Of this development there is not the slightest evidence.

4. THE TRUTH UNDERLYING UTILITARIANISM

Utilitarianism represents a onesided distortion of the fact that the good is in accord with our natural tendencies, and, therefore, pleasurable. Virtue brings peace, contentment, and happiness, safeguards bodily health, and may even prolong life. It likewise contributes to the common welfare. But these are the consequences of goodness; they indicate but do not constitute it. A bad act ordinarily breeds bad consequences, but it is not bad on their account but because in itself it constitutes a violation of the rational order.

[7] *Utilitarianism,* III.

It is a special merit of utilitarianism that it emphasizes the consequences of our actions, to which many pay little attention. Utilitarianism renders a valuable service when it insists on the duties of benevolence and demands that the good man be ever considerate of others. There are those who wrongly imagine that kindness is incompatible with authority, that the tasks they impose on others must be made disagreeable, that orders must be issued in a harsh manner, that services must not be requested but commanded, that their inferiors must be at their beck and call at all times, that their dignity does not allow them to bestow praise or to make grateful acknowledgment, that mistakes must be severely reprimanded but that the well-done performance of a task is just to be taken for granted, that under all circumstances fault must be found with the work done and that generous encouragement must never be given. Some even take upon themselves to prescribe the ways in which others should be happy. Many are so absorbed in the abstract rightness of their conduct that they do not realize how miserable they are making their entire environment. Their conviction that only their way of doing things is the right one, their intolerance of any other views, their scorn for advice, however respectfully offered, their insistence on blind obedience and their fanatic idolatry of a self-made ideal of duty become a source of irritation and resentment to everyone who has the misfortune to come into contact with them or the still greater misfortune of working for them. Such people in their conscious self-righteousness cannot understand why they are heartily disliked. In fact, their lack of imagination and sympathetic sentiment prevents them from even suspecting their utter unpopularity. Whilst their mere presence makes everybody feel uncomfortable, they yet regard themselves as paragons of virtue. A dose of utilitarianism would greatly benefit them and impart to their virtue a little more grace and humaneness. There is something radically wrong and inhuman about virtue that spreads gloom and causes uneasiness. Virtue of this type is nothing but a mask for un-adulterated selfishness. It was in reference to such virtue that a wag made the caustic remark: "Biliousness is an affection of the liver often mistaken for piety."

Utilitarianism, thus, teaches a valuable lesson. Besides recognizing the claims of sensibility in human life and making it clear that a good life can very well be enjoyable, that virtue is not self-torture and that unhappiness is no infallible index of moral perfection, it points out the great happiness value of the social impulses and the important fact that a self-centered life leads to personal impoverishment. It is also to the credit of the theory that it accentuates human equality and aims at a wide diffusion of happiness throughout the community. The greater part of what utilitarianism says about kindness and considerateness can unhesitatingly be incorporated into our own ethics. In spite of this, the fundamental defect of the system remains. Concerned only with feelings that have no abiding quality and with momentary, passing experiences, it can create no permanent moral value that will endure beyond time. Experiences are meaningless if they leave no permanent record in the character of the self.

VIII

The Moral Judgment

1. ETHICAL TRUTH

The laws of the physical world, governing the mode of operation of necessary agents, are self enforcing; the laws of the moral world, by which the activity of rational and free beings is to be regulated, become effective through the mind and the will of the agent. Man guides himself in harmony with the law and, therefore, must know it so he can apply it in the regulation of his conduct. Hence the question of the source of moral knowledge.

Knowledge of moral truths is acquired by the ordinary processes of reason. Its source is the same as that of all other knowledge. A moral principle may either be directly evident or the result of an inference. A practical moral judgment presents itself as the conclusion of an explicit or implicit syllogism. To assign any other origin to moral judgments deprives them of their objective validity and of their universal applicability. It is not in the interests of morality to try to establish a separate moral faculty, for all such attempts end in depriving morality of its rational character. The moral faculty, then, is none other than reason applied to the sphere of practical conduct. There is no moral faculty distinct from reason. Moral judgments are not a matter of blind feeling, taste, or emotional appeal, but of rational insight. A reasoned conclusion can be the only reliable standard of right and wrong. Everything else is untrustworthy and treacherous. Morality is capable of demonstration as mathematics though not with the same degree of exactitude.

Since reason is the moral guide and since, as a consequence, ethical knowledge must be laboriously acquired, it
follows that the moral notions of a time depend largely on
the stage of intellectual development which in a given
period has been reached. Even as in all other fields of knowledge men make progress, so also in the department of ethics.
We cannot look for high moral ideals and fine ethical discernment among men of low mental attainments and living
in degraded cultural environments.

In moral matters, however, reason proceeds with a spontaneity and rapidity which give to moral conclusions the
appearance of immediate intuitions. This may be explained
on the principle that nature always provides what is necessary. Under no conditions can men live in a human way
without morality, and accordingly, some guiding moral concepts must be readily available at all times. Hence Ballerini
writes in *Theologia Moralis:* "It must be admitted that there
are some practical truths necessary for the right association
of men with each other, which men feel and perceive by a
sort of rational instinct, whose proof, nevertheless, when
these same seek it analytically, they find it hard to discover.
It would seem that nature, or the author of our nature,
wished to supply the defect of the exercise of reason by an
instinct or rational sense of this kind."

2. MORAL INTUITIONISM

Intuitionism holds that moral principles are immediately
recognized as self-evident and axiomatic truths and that the
moral property of an act is perceived somewhat like a sense
quality. The theory exists in various forms and has been
proposed by Shaftesbury, Hutcheson, Cudworth, Clarke,
Butler. According to Butler conscience is a faculty of immediate moral perceptions which tells the plain man uner-
ringly and without the need of reflection the course of present duty in almost all circumstances. In this view the moral
beauty or deformity of an action are appreciated by a moral
sense after the analogy of aesthetical qualities.

The theory is contradicted by our experience which testifies to the fallibility of conscience, the hesitancy with which we make moral decisions, the laborious investigations by which we arrive at final conclusions in perplexing questions of morality and the divergence of moral judgments among men: in these there is no trace of the immediacy that accompanies sense perception and intuition. No emotional glow spontaneously bears witness to what is right and no sentimental shock automatically warns of the presence of evil.

Still moral intuitionism is right in its opposition to utilitarianism in so far as it holds that rightness is an inherent quality of certain acts and not merely something relative to and borrowed from external consequences, that it is founded in the natural order of things and possesses an unchanging eternal fitness. With us it asserts an absolute and objective morality. Thus Samuel Clarke writes: "Right and wrong are nevertheless in themselves totally and essentially different, even altogether as white and black, light and darkness."[1] The intuitionists, therefore, have signaled a vital truth, namely, that there is an absolute, eternal, and immutable element in morality.

Also it may be admitted that a normal individual whose moral nature has not been warped by evil educational influences will instinctively recoil from certain coarser forms of vice and experience an unreflective revulsion of feeling at the mere suggestion of particularly vile and ugly crimes. There are acts so grossly opposed to unspoiled moral sentiment that no reflection is necessary to realize their immoral character.

3. MORAL JUDGMENTS

Like all other judgments, moral judgments emanate from reason. They possess, however, characteristics of their own. They are addressed to the will and are pronounced with an

[1] *A Discourse Concerning the Unchangeable. Obligations of Natural Religion*, p. 50.

authoritativeness which is absent in speculative judgments. The moral *ought* not only expresses a necessary logical conclusion, but imposes itself as binding on the will. The moral judgment does not merely state a fact, but voices a command.

Moral judgments awaken strong emotional reactions because they are concerned with human values and matters of intimate personal interest. It is for that reason that so much rationalization and self-deception is practiced in the realm of morality. We feel no inclination to dispute a judgment that bears on impersonal theoretical subjects but we have some feeling about a judgment that brings home to us an obligation which possibly conflicts with our desires. In the latter instance the temptation may arise to tamper with the argument in order to evade an unpleasant conclusion. A man whose basic orientation is not moral will not be honest with himself and will make his moral judgments favor his vicious tendencies. For example, one who has an inordinate love of money will devise for himself a very strange code of honesty justifying practices which impartial reason unhesitatingly condemns. Immoral habits vitiate moral judgments and produce moral blindness.

4. CONSCIENCE

Conscience is spoken of as the voice of God. Though the phrase is a figure of speech, it is far more than an empty metaphor and possesses a real and profound significance. Conscience interprets the moral law which means that it intimates to the individual the will of God. From this fact flows the sovereign authority with which it delivers its judgments and utters its commands. It speaks with finality and demands obedience. It is the moral guide to whom we must give absolute loyalty. It possesses a sacredness which we ourselves as well as others must respect. Men claim the freedom of conscience as an inviolable right, and no earthly power may invade what has been aptly called the sanctuary of the conscience. Conscientiousness or faithfulness to the dictates of conscience is a quality to which men pay the highest homage. Not smug self-righteousness, but the approval from an enlightened and honest conscience is the greatest encouragement that can come to a man; it sustains men in their struggles for justice and comforts them in the persecutions to which they are subjected.

Literally speaking, conscience is an act of reason. More particularly, it is a practical moral judgment in the form of a reasoned conclusion by which we apply the moral law to our own acts. By it we render a decision as to what our duty is in a concrete case. It is not concerned with conduct in general, but with my own conduct at this moment and in these circumstances. It is, therefore, a very intimate and personal affair. It differs from a theoretical conclusion because it carries with it a personal reference and assumes the character of a dictate. It says: Do this! or avoid that! Since, however, we address these imperatives to ourselves, they might better be worded as follows: I must do this! or I must refrain from doing that! Conscience also reflects on acts performed or omitted, in which case it approves or condemns.

As has been noted, all moral judgments involve emotional accompaniments and are tinged with sentiment. It stands to reason that this emotional resonance will increase in proportion as the judgment comes home closer to the self. In a judgment of conscience the reference is directly personal and, accordingly, the emotional overtones will be strongly accentuated. The emotions called into play by the deliverances of conscience are awe, fear, hope, remorse, shame, regret, self-condemnation, and self-respect. If conscience approves our conduct we experience a feeling of worth and inner satisfaction; if, on the contrary, it condemns our actions, we are overwhelmed by a depressing feeling of unworth and a haunting sense of guilt and the peace of the mind is shattered. Our moral nature cowers before the tremendous utterances of conscience and in case of wrongdoing trembles like a guilty thing surprised. Obedience to

conscience is followed by confidence, serenity, and joyful-
ness; disobedience leaves in its wake uneasiness, a sense of
conviction, and a disturbing fear.

Conscience is often against our inclinations, but, though
we disobey its commands, we cannot refuse respect for we
are deeply convinced that it is on the side of the right and the
good. From this deep conviction the man who follows the
dictates of conscience draws his imperturbable assurance of
ultimate triumph for he knows that the moral forces of the
universe are with him, whereas he who defies conscience
cannot escape a premonition of defeat for he is aware that
the order of things is against him.

Contrary to the contention of Hume, conscience is not
merely the work of the heart but the work of judgment. It is
an act of reflection and has an ideational content. The feeling is present but it waits on thought. We might also de-
scribe conscience as the rational apprehension of moral
distinctions accompanied by the feeling (consciousness, conviction) of personal obligation to do what is right, or a reflective verdict of reason concerning personal conduct and evok-
ing mighty reverberations in the emotional sphere. On account of the momentous issues on which conscience bears, it
is rightly regarded as the highest function of reason.

5. THE PSYCHOLOGY OF CONSCIENCE

The phenomena of conscience are indisputable psychic
experiences, the factual reality of which no one can deny
however he may try to explain them. The portrayal of the
conflicts of conscience is a theme of stirring interest in much
of the great literature of the world. Conscience creates the
intense situations from which drama derives its powerful
appeal. The Russian novelists excel in the analysis of the
working of the guilty conscience. The annals of crime
abound with instances which illustrate the avenging power
of conscience. This stern punitive activity represents only
one, though perhaps the most startling, phase of conscience

and, incidentally gives striking testimony of man's ineradicable conviction of freedom and responsibility. It is described by Dr. J. H. Muirhead as follows: "Conscience is often pictured as a kind of judge. It carries on judicial investigations, it accuses, it bears witness, and it passes sentence. It is also executioner, seeing that it punishes with stings peculiar to itself."[2] According to whether it regards future or past actions, conscience prompts, inspires, commands, restrains or accuses, condemns, excuses, acquits. These intellectual and judicial acts are attended by appropriate emotional states. How moral judgments differ from purely speculative ones the following passage makes clear: "Another psychological characteristic of all ethical judgments is its somewhat pronounced emotional character. Men do not ordinarily affirm, this is right or that is wrong, with the coolness with which they pronounce a familiar proposition in geometry or in some matter of physical science. Judgments about matters of conduct are apt to have color, to be warmed or even to glow with feeling; and not infrequently they excite the most intense passions or the most effective enthusiasms. . . . The third psychological characteristic of ethical judgment is the peculiar relation which it sustains to the voluntary states. To judge about a matter of conduct is to establish a claim upon the will. . . . Given opportunity, judgments respecting the right and wrong of conduct become convictions of duty."[3]

The most distinctive feature connected with conscience is the consciousness of obligation, or as it is sometimes called, the feeling of "oughtness" that accompanies its dictates. This consciousness is not an inclination, nor an instinct, as Doctor Horace G. Wyatt sets forth: "Quite other is the prompting of the ought. It is not so much a drive as an inner exhortation. It is not impulsive, but imperative. And what we experience is not ourselves impelled, but ourselves impelling, ourselves impelling ourselves, indeed ourselves

---

[2] *The Elements of Ethics*, p. 72.
[3] Ladd, G. T., *Philosophy of Conduct*, Charles Scribner's Sons, N. Y., p. 117.

impelling ourselves against impulse.''[4] The necessity going
with the ought is not that of instinctive constraint but results
from the intellectual apprehension of an objective authority.
It is not the internal echo of social approval for it may
override the judgment of the community. It is not the antici-
pation of pleasure because it may run counter to our
sensual propensities and call for a sacrifice of what the
moment promises as most pleasurable. It can find no expla-
nation in our sensual nature.

6.   THE   SUPREMACY   OF   CONSCIENCE

Conscience is the moral law within us, the moral law as
reflected in the mind. Hence, it can never be lawful to go
against conscience for at the moment of acting it is, as far as
we are concerned, the moral law and the final authority.
What conscience dictates is duty for us. What it declares
good at the time being is the only good we can then and
there know and by this decision we must stand since none
other is available. It is patent that we ought to do what we
are convinced we ought to do, and it is conscience that produces this conviction. The authority of conscience cannot be
set aside.

We must follow our conscience even if it renders an erroneous decision, which, owing to man's limitations, is a
possible contingency. Obedience is necesasry because for the
agent, who is unaware of the error, the false judgment is
nevertheless authentic and authoritative, and he honestly
thinks that he is following the right lead. Whilst, therefore,
fidelity to conscience may mislead one to do what is wrong,
this remains exceptional and, when some criminal deed has
been committed, we may be practically certain that it is not
the outcome of acting in conformity with conscience but
rather acting contrary to it. As a rule the decisions of the
normal conscience are correct. Moreover, one who habitually
respects his conscience and trusts to it for guidance in his
conduct will be inclined to keep it well informed.

[4] *The Art of Feeling*, p. 169.

To be safe guides of action, the answers which conscience returns must be clear and certain. He who acts in doubt willingly takes the risk of offending against the law. Before acting the doubt must be dispelled and conscience properly formed. Where this cannot be achieved by direct investigation, we may fall back on the reflex principle that a doubtful law does not bind. A law may be regarded as doubtful if a solidly probable reason militates against it. This indirect solution of doubt is called probabilism, which must always be cautiously employed. It cannot be applied where a definite end must be attained or certain consequences absolutely avoided.

7. THE EDUCATION OF CONSCIENCE

The role of conscience as the supreme moral guide makes its proper training a vital necessity, lest it become a guide unto destruction. We render our moral discernment expedite, reliable, sure and keen by the faithful study of moral principles, by the cultivation of lofty moral ideals, by the association with high-minded and conscientious people, and by reading the lives of men noted for their mortal integrity. Acting according to the light we have received will help us toward a fuller and clearer vision of duty. Thus George Tyrrell writes: "It is then by fidelity to the light which is in us, and by availing ourselves of the means of instruction provided for us, that we may hope ever to progress toward a greater refinement in our power of moral judgment."[5]

Conscience can deteriorate and decay to an alarming degree, and this in men whose minds in other respects function normally. Rationalization and misuse take the edge off conscience. A conscience thus rendered dull and unresponsive is termed a seared conscience and signals a truly sad moral state. It is doubtful, though, if conscience can be reduced to complete atrophy as long as a glimmering of sanity remains. A man in whom conscience no longer stirred would have to

[5] *Hard Sayings*, p. 56.

be looked upon as a moral monstrosity. A not exceptional phenomenon, however, is a conscience that has been silenced and muzzled with regard to certain categories of moral wrong but which manifests an oversensitiveness toward other forms. Slackness in one direction is quite compatible with excessive scrupulosity in another. The scrupulosity in this case serves as a compensatory mechanism and a mask.

The process of the decline of conscience is well described by Father Henry Keane, S.J., as follows: "Apart from the failure of the reasoning powers, there are two main causes of a relaxed grasp of moral principles. The first is action in direct opposition to them. (The sin against the light.) A man can accustom himself very easily to act against his better judgment. After some time this judgment hardly asserts itself at all, till he ends by taking true for false and false for true. This is what Plato called the lie in the soul and justly regarded it as one of the greatest calamities that can befall man. . . . The second and most potent agent of decay is the influence of passion, the 'charm that steals the wits even of the wise.' In practice these two work together."[6]

8. PRUDENCE

The virtue which aids conscience in making the right moral decisions is prudence. It is practical wisdom which directs us to choose the right values and to observe due measure in all things. Without it the other virtues become distorted. Good will is not enough and indiscreet zeal may cause much harm. Prudence counsels to seek advice when one's own knowledge is inadequate. Stubbornly to rely on one's own resources and to refuse the help of the wise in the formation of one's conscience bespeaks folly. Prudence is the fruit of sincere striving, of self-discipline and of loving contemplation of the law of God. Opposed to prudence are carnal wisdom, worldly prudence, and sophistication.

[6] Keane, Rev. Henry, S.J., *A Primer of Moral Philosophy*, P. J. Kenedy Co., N. Y., p. 104.

9. THE POWER OF CONSCIENCE

Conscience is a powerful factor in life because it produces an intense conviction of duty and mobilizes our emotions in the service of righteousness. It can make heroes and saints. An aroused conscience is the greatest moral force in the universe, it shrinks from no obstacle and cringes before no earthly power. It does not rest until it has overcome evil. If a man loses confidence in the justice of his position, he no longer has the courage to defend it. On the other hand, unconquerable is the man whose conscience unwaveringly testifies to the righteousness of his cause.

A peaceful conscience is man's greatest treasure. By the same token, a disturbed conscience can become a source of untold misery, precipitate torturing inner conflicts, and result in the most agonizing mental sufferings. The right guidance of conscience, therefore, is a very important element in mental hygiene.

IX

Universality of Moral Notions

1. MORALITY A RATIONAL PHENOMENON

Morality growing out of man's rational constitution is inseparable from man. A recognition of a moral distinction between different kinds of action is as universal as humanity itself. In the lowest condition of life as it exists among savages, we find an acceptation of some limitation to action besides that of physical capacity or external restraint. A moral man who is unaware of the distinction between good and evil and knows of no obligation is a pure myth. The basic principles by which men regulate their conduct are essentially alike though there is considerable difference in the application. This justifies W. M. Wundt in saying in his *Ethics:* "Man has always had the same kind of moral endowment." Not only, therefore, is there a universal moral consciousness among men but there exists likewise a stock of common norms of conduct bearing on fundamental human relations. To this L. T. Hobhouse testifies: "The comparative study of ethics, which is apt in its earlier stages to impress the student with a bewildering sense of the diversity of moral judgments, ends rather by impressing him with a fundamental and far-reaching uniformity. Through the greatest extent of time and space over which we have records, we find a recurrence of the common features of ordinary morality, which to my mind at least is not less impressive than the variations which also appear."[1] Sweeping generalizations as the following, therefore, are not warranted: "Conscience codes are as typical and characteristic products of social evolution as languages or political systems."[2]

That any tribe devoid of moral notion can be found is denied by J. L. A. de Qautrefages: "Confining ourselves rigorously to the region of facts, and carefully avoiding the territory of philosophy and theology, we may state without hesitation that there is no human society, or even association in which the idea of good and evil is not represented by certain acts regarded by the members as morally good or morally bad."[3] Bishop A. LeRoy, who lived among the most primitive tribes of Africa, writes to the same purport: "To restrict ourselves at once to those populations with whom alone we are concerned here, and who, be it constantly borne in mind, figure among the least advanced in the whole world, we bear witness to what is indeed a most outstanding fact. Namely, that though their languages — generally well provided with verbs and nouns — are exceedingly scant in adjectives, yet adjectives are never wanting to characterize what is good and what is bad, what is true or false, just or unjust."[4] Later on in the same work the author remarks: "One thing however should be noted. Although the principle itself of justice, together with the definite concept of good and bad, is the very base of the entire moral life of the Blacks, and indeed of the Primitives in general, yet the practical application they make of it to the details of their own actions is often deplorably erroneous." In view of such reliable testimony the opinion of Sir J. Lubbock may be set aside: "While even the lowest savages have many material and intellectual attainments they are, it seems to me, almost entirely wanting in moral feeling."[5]

[1] Hobhouse, L. T., *Morals in Evolution*, H. Holt and Co., N. Y., Vol. I, 11.
[2] Hayes, E. C., *Sociology and Ethics*, p. 184.
[3] *L'Espèce Humaine*, XXXIV.
[4] *La Religion des Primitifs*.
[5] *Origin of Civilization*.

On the other hand, since moral ideals, standards, and customs result from the use of reason, there is room both for
variability and progress. Moral judgment can be more or less
refined and this will manifest itself in the moral customs of
the time. These variations, however, remain within certain
limits so that a certain common pattern is always discernible
in the different moral codes. There are actions (filial devotion) which are always recognized as good and others (adultery, incest) which are always branded as evil. Throughout
history the number of virtues and sins has substantially re-
mained the same. Rational development plays an essential
part in the application of the moral principles to ever widening circles and newly arising situations. Thus we may sum
up the matter in the words of Bishop LeRoy: "And we conclude that if philosophers like Kant, Condorcet, Buckle, and
others have established that the basis of morality is identical,
universal and inborn in man, the attentive and comparative
study of the Primitives proves that these men have reason
for their contention. And yet Pascal, in turn, was not more
wrong than they in his aphorism that ran: 'Truth on this
side of the Pyrenees, error on the other.' What Pascal had in
mind was the applications men made of the principles of
morality. Of these applications, and of these only, may one
be permitted to affirm that they belong to any given place or
time."[6]

2. ORIGIN OF MORAL PRINCIPLES

Rightly we speak of a moral endowment of man, which,
on the affective side, consists chiefly of the emotions of shame
and sympathy and, on the intellectual side, of a ready apprehension of primary moral principles. These general
moral principles, practical application of which is made by
conscience, are acquired and the habitual grasp of them is
known as synderesis. Such basic principles would be: we must

[6] *Op. cit.*

do what is good, avoid evil, reverence the Supreme Being, respect our rational nature, show gratitude, obey parents, shun injustice, refrain from lying, love our neighbors. Moral progress consists in the numerical increase of such principles, in a greater clarification and better understanding of their content and in an extension of their application to ever widening circles. Thus the concept of the neighbor enlarges until it embraces the whole race and all limitation of duties to members of a special group disappears. Tribal morality expands into universal morality. Hence, the racialism of our times, which again narrows the concept of the neighbor, is a retrogression to lower levels of moral development.

As a matter of fact we are born into an ethically organized environment and enter upon a rich moral inheritance. We do not need to elaborate a moral code for ourselves but it comes to us by way of tradition, education, and social control and is accepted on the strength of parental and social authority. At this first stage our moral ideas have the form of beliefs. As the reflective judgment grows, they deepen into intellectual convictions held in virtue of their own intrinsic evidence. At this second stage assent is prompted by logical insight and rational understanding. The change may be effected by a gradual transition or may be brought about by a sudden critical experience. At all events, when the authoritative basis of morality gives way to the questionings of critical reflection a rational underpinning must be supplied. If this is done at the right time, the so-called moral revolt of the adolescent generation against what they consider arbitrary restraints and outmoded traditions will be forestalled.

When the child begins to realize itself as a self among other selves, the stage for moral training in the proper sense is set. The conflicts which the child experiences with its own impulses and the friction which it encounters with its environment, furnish opportunities for moral formation. It is under these circumstances that the sense of justice and considerateness is born. Unguided, the moral life of the child cannot be unified, though even at a very early age isolated acts of moral virtue may be expected. At the age of twelve children give evidence of a very definite moral consciousness. The ideas of wrong and duty in the childhood stage are identified with the forbidden and the commanded, and accordingly obedience is the special virtue of this period. Early morality is chiefly by habit, later it is reduced to principles. Religion is a very potent factor in awakening and strengthening the moral sense.[7]

3. THE PRESENT-DAY MORAL REVOLT

There is in our days considerable talk of a new morality and the ethical teachings of the past are violently assailed as no longer in harmony with the requirements of social and economic life. The movement received a special impulse from Nietzsche's demand for the "Transmutation of all values." The tendency to revise tradition, to re-examine the foundations of accepted beliefs and to destroy what was held sacred by previous generations, while a common phenomenon in our days, is particularly noticeable in the field of ethical truth. Moral iconoclasm is quite the fashion.

The challenge must be met. No age is supposed to accept uncritically the traditions of preceding generations. However, legitimate criticism is something very different from wholesale repudiation. It is folly to think that our age is the first to discover real wisdom and that the best for us to do is to assign to the scrapheap the intellectual and moral treasures of the past which may contain much that is of lasting value. To review the causes of the modern revolt will be our first task.

The exaggerated individualism of our times must be regarded as its main source. Every man looks upon himself as the supreme arbiter of truth and right regardless of the inherent limitations of private judgment and the numerous

[7] Cf. McGrath, Marie Cecilia, Ph.D., *A Study of the Moral Development of Children;* Hull, E. R., S.J., *The Formation of Character.*

subjective interferences with the reasoning processes. This has led to intellectual and moral chaos which in its turn has made man think that there are no objective moral standards. As a result everyone framed for himself a moral code which suited his fancy and which was largely a product of his undisciplined passions. Men who are prone to criticize everything else but too frequently forget to criticize their own competence and so succumb to the vagaries of an untrained mind, following really the subtle suggestions of selfishness when they flatter themselves that they are obeying the laws of objective and impartial thinking. This becomes evident when we consider the quality of the new morality, which reveals itself not as an advance to higher and purer forms of human conduct but as an ignominious retreat from the heights which humanity has laboriously conquered. In some cases, it is quite manifest that the so-called new morality constitutes nothing but a cowardly compromise with man's lower animal instincts. Of this the surrender of the monogamous and indissoluble marriage is the most obvious instance. The new morality is characterized by laxity, irresponsibility and lack of self-discipline. It is devoid of heroic elements and presents an attitude of abject defeatism.

In many circles morality was imposed in a purely authoritarian fashion with no rational insight into the meaning of moral laws and had become overlaid with numerous arbitrary prohibitions of a conventional nature. Puritanical rigorism had given to moral laws the appearance of capricious restrictions on liberty without any internal justification. Falsely morality came to be identified with what was called the tyranny of custom, from which men sought to emancipate themselves. Unfortunately, in the opposition which arose against that which was artificial in the prevailing morality the legitimate essential kernel was rejected with the external husk. This happened the more readily as the arbitrary conventional aspects had frequently been emphasized with greater insistence than the underlying essentials.

Ultraconservative resistance to needed revisions of accepted moral positions brought discredit to the whole moral system. This occurred particularly in the realm of economics in which the liberalistic ideas of property were defended as absolute moral categories. The persistent abuse of property rights resulted in a denial of the fundamental human right of ownership. When morality is used to bolster up class privilege it can no longer command universal respect and allegiance.

At times a revision and revaluation of social customs may be really required in the name and in the interests of true morality. As a matter of fact, the Church leads in this fight for purer moral ideals and practical applications of the moral law more in harmony with growing enlightenment. The modern revolt, however, proceeds from false premises, is inspired by wrong motives and sins by excess. Its basis of moral positivism and evolutionism is scientifically unsound. It would land us in universal moral skepticism and bring upon us utter moral chaos and anarchy. Adherence to a narrow and repressive code will be less harmful than the total absence of definite moral standards. Moral anarchism will play havoc with human happiness and the casting off of all restraint will reduce life to a state of disgusting crudity. Past generations were not so unlike ourselves that the rules which they adopted would be entirely unsuitable to us. There is something unchanging in human nature and morality is the expression of man's profoundest and most universal needs.

Immoralism must be combated and halted before its destructive influence spreads and leaves nothing but wreckage. Morality is the dam that stems the devastating flood of uncontrolled passion and without it individual and social life are jeopardized. When a society becomes honeycombed with the rage of unrestrained self-expression, its doom is not far distant. Hardship and oppression can strengthen a nation and prepare it for a glorious destiny but no nation can survive widespread immorality. Human happiness and social progress are bound up with morality.

4. CONVENTIONAL   RULES   OF   CONDUCT

The impression that morality is merely of temporary and
local validity arises when the distinction between morals and
manners becomes blurred. The confusion is sometimes deliberately fostered by the advocates of the new morality in
order to strengthen their case. Though in some respects
morality and conventionality are alike, no impartial observer
can fail to notice their essential difference. The frequent re-
ferences in our days of sophistication to the Victorian age
bear on the artificial and somewhat hypocritical conventions
of that period, which was more concerned with outward respectability than solid virtue.

Conventions lack the universality of moral customs and
are identified with certain social strata whose external prestige they are intended to preserve. Such are the code of
honor of the military caste and the ideal of the gentleman.
They are differentiated from moral rules by the degree of
obligation felt toward their fulfillment, the kind of feeling
evoked by their violation, the character of the sanctions by
which they are enforced, the range of the persons they affect
and their relative permanence. Conventions are considered
to be less binding and authoritative than morals and are often
set aside by men of high moral ideals. Conformity to conventions is not regarded as virtue and contempt for conventions is looked upon as eccentricity but not branded as immorality. A violation of a conventual rule may produce extreme mortification and chagrin, momentarily very acute,
but reflection does not allow remorse and moral self-condemnation to arise. Some carry the devotion to the conventions of their social class to absurd lengths and allow it to
interfere with true moral duties, especially that of charity.
There is a type of hypocrisy which values conformity to conventional standards higher than moral rectitude. Such unreasonable insistence on the importance and obligatory
character of conventions may discredit not only them but
morals as well.

5. THE USES OF CONVENTIONS

Conventions are forms which regulate the externals of social intercourse. By restraining the impulsive spontaneity of behavior they lift human relations into an atmosphere of dignity, prevent friction, and render mutual contacts more agreeable. They surround us with what we designate as the proprieties, decencies and amenities without which life would lose its charm. They burgeon into such beautiful things as reserve and reticence. They are not purely arbitrary but grow out of the requirements of human dignity and the exigencies of social life. The realm of sex, in which unrestrained spontaneity is particularly dangerous and likely to undermine mutual respect, has been hedged about with many conventual safeguards which cannot be disregarded with impunity. Bohemianism, which exalts the life untrammeled by conventions, neither provides the soil in which virture thrives nor does it make for greater pleasantness and happiness, though its adherents try to make themselves believe that it does. Life is a delicate flower and if handled by uncouth hands loses its bloom. Freed from conventions it becomes crude and vulgar.

With regard to morality, the function of conventions is protective. Around the inner citadel they create a safety zone and ward off the first attack. With true insight into their psychological significance they are sometimes referred to as minor morals. "Manners," says Dr. Samuel S. Drury, "are the protecting armor of morals and when manners are abandoned nature is rudely exposed."[8] When the conventional restraints have gone by the board, the first defenses have been surrendered.

From the preceding we conclude that conventions should neither be despised as useless and hypocritical nor overvalued as ends in themselves. Whilst there are customs which are "more honored in the breach than the observance," the

[8] *The Influence of the Church on Modern Problems*, p. 19.

general attitude toward established customs should be one of respect, for conventions do not long outlive their inherent usefulness but, even after this has gone, they usually retain some ornamental value. Unconventionality for its own sake has nothing to commend it. Dr. J. S. MacKenzie's suggestions will prove helpful: "Besides the commandments, or strict moral laws, we find in every community a number of subordinate rules of conduct, inferior in authority, but often superior in the obedience which they elicit. We ought not to slight these narrow conventional laws; for they were originally invented as a safeguard against various forms of wrong and injustice."[9]

The sensible teacher of ethics will be careful not to invest mere conventional customs, useful as they may be, with an authoritativeness which belongs only to moral laws, nor to brand as immoral every deviation from the rules of conventional conduct, provided morality is not undermined and virtue seriously endangered. Those who think it grand to shock others by their provocative unconventionality might profitably be made to see that their technique is crude and their behavior silly rather than wicked. To take offense in such cases is doing too much honor to a childish effort to obtain the limelight. If oftener we called the fool a fool, instead of flattering his ego and dignifying him by calling him a knave, we should sooner see him reform or at least subside.

[9] MacKenzie, Dr. J. S., *Manual of Ethics,* Noble and Noble Co., N. Y., p. 342.

X

The Moral Order

1. THE DISTINCTION BETWEEN GOOD AND EVIL

By a logical transition the preceding chapter leads to the present inquiry dealing with the nature and the reason of the difference between good and evil, for, if as we have seen moral distinctions are unanimously accepted, there must be something to account for this unanimity and at the same time a common criterion, in reference to which these distinctions are made, must be available.

Contrary to Moral Positivism there exists between moral good and evil an internal and essential difference, which has an anchorage in the very structure of human acts and is not superimposed on them either by positive enactment or any adventitious circumstance. Some acts are inherently good because they harmonize with the fitness of things, others are in their innermost tendencies bad because they represent some radical incompatibility with the order of the cosmic scheme. The distinction between good and evil grows out of life itself and expresses its deepest exigencies. With an absolute conviction men hold that benevolent affections are superior to malevolent ones, truth to falsehood, justice to injustice, gratitude to ingratitude, chastity to sensuality, loyalty to treachery. Accordingly W. E. H. Lecky justly asserts: "No one who desires to become holier and better imagines that he does so by becoming more malevolent, or more untruthful, or more unchaste. Everyone who desires to attain perfection in these departments of feeling is impelled toward benevolence, toward veracity, toward chastity."[1] We realize that there is something so inherently proper, fitting and becoming in mercy, temperance, piety, that they will always be regarded as virtues and can never be converted into vices. If nothing can blot out the distinction, it must be rooted in the nature of things.

If the difference between good and evil springs from the essence of things and their relations in the cosmic order, there is no mystery about it and it is ascertainable by reason. Hence, as soon as man understands his own nature and the place which he occupies in the order of the universe, it becomes clear to him what this nature and his position require of him; he sees what befits this nature and what is in conformity with its native tendencies. No one will deny that it is good to bring nature to its fullest fruition and to live according to what is best, finest, and highest in our nature. Any other course appears as unworthy of a rational being. Even Utilitarianism emphatically declares that "it is better to be a human being dissatisfied than a pig satisfied; better to be Socrates dissatisfied than a fool satisfied." The moment man recognizes the hierarchical order of his faculties, it becomes manifest to him that the nobler should rule over the lower. Likewise, when he realizes that he is essentially social, he understands that it is proper for him to adapt himself to life in society. It is impossible for man to see anything commendable in the degradation of his nature and in brutalizing himself. He may choose the path of unrestrained sensuality but, in doing so, he feels that he has lowered himself. Whilst choosing the contrary alternative, he still is persuaded that the better choice would be the full development of his being in that order and proportion which nature has intended.

[1] *Op. cit.,* I, p. 100.

2. T H E   N O R M   O F   M O R A L I T Y

The moral good is the natural good transposed to the sphere of free human activity. This is not a static but a dynamic universe in which all things, particularly living beings, are endowed with potentialities of development and strive for fulfillment and richer being. All seek the things conducive to this purpose and shun what is prejudicial. By dint of internal necessity the dumb creation is infallibly directed toward its proper good and end. Man, capable of self-direction, must discover for himself what is good for him and intelligently and of free choice seek it. The moral good, hence, is the natural good of man deliberately sought. It is this view, according to which the moral good is an aspect of the natural good, that links the moral good to the demands, exigencies, and strivings of human nature and makes of it an object of appetency and desire. The right understanding of this view will make us see in morality something eminently natural. Just as it is good for a tree to be planted in fertile soil, so it is good for man to lead the moral life for only such a life furnishes the conditions of full human development.

Modern ethics has too much separated the moral good from the natural good and made of it something mystical, artificial, and remote. Thus morality came to be identified rather with the suppression of desire and the negation of inner tendencies than with the fulfillment of all that is truly human. Modern ethics divorced moral goodness from happiness and placed them in opposition, whereas there exists between the two the closest relation. The Greek mind in this respect proved more penetrating when it made the good, not law nor duty, the chief category of ethics and stressed the attractiveness rather than the imperativeness of the moral ideal. When morality addresses itself to the will it must take the form of law and duty, but the content of duty and law is not at all foreign to our nature but expressive of

its real tendencies. For the will the good is law and duty, for
the unspoiled heart it is exactly what would be wanted and
desired. Take the commandment which imposes on children
the duty to love their parents; well, that is precisely what
children want to do in response to the natural inclination
of the heart.

The moderns make great show of pleading for a scientific,
natural morality, which is based on human needs, consults
experience, observes the results of conduct, contributes to
human happiness, and can be justified by reason. Nothing
could be more sensible, and to construct a system of ethics
answering to these specifications has ever been the aim of
Scholastic philosophy. So St. Thomas says: "What pertains
to moral science is known mostly through experience."[2] The
practical and realistic character of Scholastic Ethics is evi-
denced by the fact that it makes human nature the norm of
morality. What is good for man must be learned from the
study of man.

Every being carries in its nature, which is the source of its
tendencies and activities, the law of its own development,
the pattern of what it should become. It strives toward the
actualization of its innate potentialities. The objects which
minister to this end are good, those which defeat it are bad.
The measure of goodness is the fitness of an object or an act
to satisfy the innate tendencies of a being and to promote
the perfection foreshadowed in its structure.

Applied to man this rule reads: That is good for man
which befits human nature and suits it in its most distinctive
characteristics. Now, since there exists in man certain permanent natural strivings and tendencies which belong inseparably to his human endowment, there also exist certain
objects answering to these strivings. These are essentially
good. The distinction between good and bad, accordingly,
is as immutable as human nature itself, the standard, the

[2] *Ethicorum*, I, 3.

norm, the criterion or the rule by which it is determined. As
Macbeth declares:

> I dare do all that may become a man;
> Who dares do more, is none.

The human self, however, is a complex being, and the
good, therefore, is not that which corresponds to part of his
nature but that which is required by his nature as a whole.
To be the norm of morality human nature must be taken
adequately, in all its aspects and all its relations.

In his constitution man is spiritual and sensual. His nature
must be regarded as a hierarchy of powers and faculties with
different degrees of dignity. Reason demands that between
these different faculties an appropriate order be observed.
From this we deduce man's duties relative to himself.

Man stands in an essential relation of dependence to his
Maker, from which man's duties toward God are derived.

Likewise man is a social being and this aspect of his nature
gives rise to his duties toward his fellow men and society.
Thus, human nature adequately conceived constitutes a
norm that can be applied to all human activities, and surely
no one could claim that it is an arbitrary, artificial, external,
or merely conventional standard.

3. MORALITY AND HUMAN WELFARE

A moral code framed in accord with the norm set forth
cannot but be in every way beneficial and conducive to the
well-being of the individual as well as society. If morally
good acts are those which are in conformity with human nature, they necessarily contribute to man's proper growth,
the fuller realization of his personality and a more abundant
and happier life. They must likewise make for better mutual
relations among men, order, peace, and social welfare. On
the other hand, the immoral, being contrary to human
nature, must be harmful and happiness destroying. It is also
unsocial and antisocial.

Since morality consists in conformity with human nature it coincides with the general good of man. As a result there exists a profound harmony between moral laws and the basic needs of human nature, which extends even to the biological requirements of human existence. Mental and physical health are fostered by obedience to the moral laws and nothing favors mental breakdown and physical disintegration more than certain vices. This need not surprise us if we keep in mind that morality, springing from the very depths of human nature, is in essence the expression of the highest laws of life. Psychology and medicine regard faithfulness to the moral laws as a favorable factor in the maintenance of bodily vigor and mental soundness. As the etymology of the words indicates there exists between health and holiness a closer relation than is usually suspected.[3]

On the basis of the preceding we can establish a secondary or derivative criterion of morality, taken respectively from the good or bad consequences of acts. A course of conduct which as a rule is fraught with injurious consequences must be pronounced morally bad, whilst a policy productive of beneficent results reveals itself as morally good. The rule, however, works only when we adopt a long-range view for in immediate experience things do no always turn out that way. It may take a long time before the detrimental consequences even of habitual wrongdoing become manifest. Dishonesty may successfully be practiced for many years. Similar is the case with regard to birth control, the deleterious effects of which, such as marital unhappiness, injury to health, breaking up of home life, increase in the divorce rate, decrease of the population and eventually race suicide, are observable only after a considerable lapse of time. Nor can the rule safely be applied to individual acts for a lie in a particular case may really prove profitable and bring great advantages. Beneficial or injurious consequences, therefore,

[3] Cf. Hadfield, J. A., *Psychology and Morals;* Walsh, Dr. J. J., *Religion and Health;* Foerster, Dr. F. W., *Marriage and the Sex Problem.*

can neither function as a decisive and handy criterion of good and evil nor act as an effective deterrent from wrong-doing. Besides the criterion in question is not constitutive but merely manifestative. Hence, if no evil consequences should ensue the act would still be bad.

4. THE   ULTIMATE   NORM

Man is created in the image of his Maker, and, hence, the ultimate norm of morality is the Divine Nature. Moral goodness is the reflection of God's own holiness. Accordingly, morality brings out in man the divine pattern and makes him godlike. Immorality blurs and finally obliterates in him the divine likeness.

In the light of this truth the maxim of Ethical Culture, respect human dignity in yourself and others, takes on a fresh and sublime meaning for, according to this view, man possesses a sacramental character inasmuch as he participates in the divine likeness. Degradation of human nature is in this case a species of desecration, a profanation of something sacred. It is essential that man have an exalted idea of himself for if men have a low estimate of themselves they are likely to conduct themselves accordingly. A sense of dignity is a mighty preservative and exerts an upward gravitational pull on man's actions; it imparts a sharp fillip to the will.

Economic exploitation, which so frequently leads to a stunting of human nature and a degradation of human personality, when gauged by this doctrine appears as an intolerable crime. The same holds true of any mistreatment or oppression of a human being. The greater the dignity we ascribe to human beings, the more unendurable will it appear to see them abused and reduced to an unworthy condition of destitution or dependence. We feel that something inviolable has been outraged.

The doctrine of the divine likeness of man enables us to appreciate the full import of the indictment of modern industry stated by Pius XI in *Quadragesimo Anno:* "And so bodily labor, which was decreed by Providence for the good of man's body and soul even after original sin, has everywhere been changed into an instrument of strange perversion; for dead matter leaves the factory ennobled and transformed, where men are corrupted and degraded."

5. A SCALE OF VALUES

Moral values are not of our subjective creation but objective goods existing independently of our own preference. They are to be judged by an objective standard, namely their appropriateness to fit in with the essential tendencies of our nature. We can, therefore, construct a scale of values which should guide us in our practical choices. There are interests that occupy the highest place in the scale and which may never be sacrificed. The supremacy of certain values is expressed in the Gospel: "For what doth it profit a man, if he gain the whole world and suffer the loss of his own soul?" (Matt. 16:26.) There are things, the gain of which will have to be looked upon as a loss; there are other things for which no price is too high.

St. Thomas explains how we ascertain what is good for man: "There are certain activities naturally suited to man, and these activities are in themselves right and not merely by positive law. . . . It is natural to man to be a social being. Those things, therefore, naturally befit man without which the maintenance of human society would be impossible. . . . The use of lower creatures to meet the need of human life is a natural property of man. Now there is a certain measure in which the use of aforesaid creatures is helpful to human life. If this measure is transgressed, as in the disorderly taking of food, it results in harm to man and is inappropriate. In the natural order, man's body is for his soul, and the lower powers of the soul for reason. It is therefore naturally right for man so to manage his body and lower faculties of his soul so that the good of reason may be helped. . . . To every man those things are befitting, whereby he

tends to his natural end; and the contraries are naturally un-
befitting. But God is the end to which man is ordained by
nature. Those things therefore are naturally right, whereby
man is led to the knowledge and love of God."[4]

[4] *Contra Gentiles*, III, 129.

XI

The Moral Law

---

1. THE GOOD AS DUTY (DEONTOLOGY)

There is something compelling about the moral good. It not only attracts but lays compulsion on us. It connotes constraint and necessity. It is experienced as a duty. This imperious compulsion with which the moral good confronts us, though not a physical coercion, is a real necessity which addresses itself to the will conscious of its freedom of choice. It is an imperative ought, a supreme command. The good, thus, appears not merely as a desirable ideal which I may realize according to my own pleasure but as a law that demands fulfillment. It is impossible to divest the good of this obligatory character which is always and strikingly in evidence. Man feels bound, held, constrained to do what he recognizes as right. For ethics it is a vital question how the good comes to take on this quality of obligatoriness.

What is befitting man can be ascertained by a study of human nature as has been previously explained. Man appears as possessed of a personal dignity and certain acts are experienced as an outrage against his nature. There are acts which he cannot but brand as unbecoming and degrading, acts of which reason cannot approve. There are other lines of conduct which appeal to his rational self and in which he sees an ennobling quality. Still, this justifies us only in calling such modes of behavior decent, proper, worthy of man, conformed to rational demand, but does not allow us to pronounce them obligatory. What if man wants to dishonor his nature, insult his reason and lower himself to the level of the brute,

That man may not act in this fashion and wantonly debase himself we prove from the fact that his nature created in the likeness of the Divinity has an infinite worth stamped upon it, that he is not his own master, that he has an exalted destiny and that he is subject to a higher will whose holiness and goodness command absolute reverence. The will of God makes the good an inviolable duty. Behind duty stands the awful majesty of the Divinity. The notion of duty, then, presupposes the idea of God as the supreme Ruler of the universe. It can neither logically arise nor acquire its full weight unless we recognize the existence of one who is impelled by the necessity of his own essence infinitely perfect to will the right order, who in virtue of its absolute holiness may impose his will unconditionally on the created universe, and who by reason of his title as Creator has both the right to exact and the power to enforce obedience to his holy laws.

2.   THE   SACREDNESS   OF   DUTY

If duty has its source in the holy will of God, its august character becomes immediately manifest. We understand why men speak of it in terms of highest respect and why loyalty to duty enjoys the greatest esteem. Kant's apostrophe does not exaggerate: "Duty! Thou sublime and mighty name that dost embrace nothing charming or insinuating, but requirest submission, and yet seekest not to move the will by threatening aught that would arouse natural aversion or terror, but merely holdest forth a law which of itself finds entrance into the mind, and yet gains reluctant reverence (though not always obedience), a law before which all inclinations are dumb, even though they secretly counterwork it; what origin is there worthy of thee, and where is to be found the root of thy noble descent which proudly rejects all kindred with the inclinations; a root such that to be derived

from it is the indispensable condition of the only worth
which men can give themselves?"[1] True, all personal worth
of man comes from the fulfillment of his duties and he deserves honor in proportion as he adheres steadfastly to the
course of duty. In the measure that he proves untrue to
duty, he also forfeits his own self-respect. Poets glorify duty.
Thus Wordworth in *Ode to Duty:*

> Stern Daughter of the Voice of God!
> O Duty! If that name thou love
> Who art a light to guide, a rod
> To check the erring and reprove;
> Thou, who art victory and law
> When empty terrors overawe;
> From vain temptations dost set free;
> And calmst the weary strife of frail humanity!

A life devoted to duty is not a life sacrificed to a phantom
nor a life blighted by senseless repressions. Duty is the best
guide for impulsive and capricious man; it steadies him and
protects the interests of his future self against the lure of
the moment. It steers him into the right path when his
sensual inclinations and the clamorous demands of selfishness are at cross purposes. Duty is not alien to our nature nor
hostile to human inclinations. It does not aim at a stoical
extirpation of emotions and affections but integrates them
with moral purposes. There is a fanaticism of duty which
would banish beauty, joy, and happiness from this earth
and render human life drab, dreary, and ungenerous. This
is a distortion of the concept of duty and at variance with
the true notion of morality.

The moral ought is absolute and unconditional. It is a
categorical imperative which admits of no alternatives and
removes every conceivable "if." Many an *ought* confronts us
in life but the necessity which they impose is linked to a condition or end which we are at liberty to accept or reject. No
condition, no weakening "if" or "unless," is attached to the

[1] *Critique of Practical Reason*, I, 1, 3.

moral *ought,* which is bound to the supreme end that may not be set aside. We are brought face to face with the Eternal God and the ultimate realities.

3. THE NATURAL LAW

Duty stems from the will of God and his law to which the entire creation is subject. Law rules this world because it has been brought into existence by an Intelligent Being in order to realize a purpose. In the physical world law works through mechanical necessity, in the rational world by means of obligation. Obligation, which moves the free will in a manner consentaneous with its nature, is the formal effect of law; hence, duty and law are correlative.

The law is a rule of action; it guides and directs, producing order and harmony. In the absence of law chaos, confusion, and finally destruction would ensue. Such a state of affairs cannot have been the intention of the Creator when he planned the universe, and so the law governing the universe must be coeternal in the mind of God with the decision to create. This law is defined by St. Augustine as "the Divine Reason and Will commanding that the natural order of things be preserved and forbidding that it be disturbed."

The natural law is the eternal law, which encompasses the entire creation, applied to the realm of rational and free agents. The law is for the benefit of those whom it obligates. To deny the existence of the natural law, that is a law for the human world, is to say that God has left the world of rational beings without proper guidance and inadequately provided for them. It would exclude man from participation in the eternal will of God to order. The absence of a law for man would bespeak a radically defective world neglecting those who rank highest in the visible universe. There must, accordingly, be a natural law securing in the world of men the same beneficent order which prevails throughout the rest of the universe. Out of this natural law arises duty, because it could not become effective and would remain futile with-

out obligation. God decrees that man should act in conformity with the requirements of his nature, and the will of
the Creator is the law of the creature. Both the good of man
and the wisdom of God demand the existence of the natural
law.

The sublimity of the law depends on the object at which it
aims, the range of its application and the quality of the will
from which it emanates. Now, the natural law aims at the
highest good of man, it extends its protection to all mankind
without exception and it has its source in the holy will of the
infinitely wise and good God, a fact which guarantees its
eminently rational and beneficent character. The contemplation of this law elicits from Kant this beautiful tribute:
"Two things fill the mind with ever new and increasing ad-
miration, the oftener and the more steadily we reflect on
them: the starry heavens above and the moral law within."
And the Psalmist reverently exclaims: "The law of the Lord
is unspotted." (Ps. 18:8). Submission to this law is not slavish
obsequiousness, because reason tells us that both on account
of its origin and its effect it is worthy of obedience.

4. KNOWLEDGE OF THE NATURAL LAW

That there is a law anterior to all human statutes has been
held throughout the ages. Sir W. Blackstone refers to these
decrees as follows: "These are the eternal, immutable laws of
good and evil to which the Creator Himself, in all His dis-
pensations, conforms; and which He has enabled human
reason to discover, so far as they are necessary for the conduct of human actions."[2] Antigone in Sophocles' tragedy refuses to obey the King's order in the name of this higher law:

It was not Zeus above who framed that law,
Nor justice whispering from the underworld.
Nor deemed I thy decrees were of such force
As to override the sanctities of heaven —

[2] *Commentaries on the Laws of England.*

> Which are not of today, nor yesterday.
> From whom, whence they first issued, no
>   man knows.

These laws, since they are not arbitrary but the outcome
of the exigencies of human nature, have always been known
by mankind in proportion to their necessity. The primary
dictates without which human life could not go on have
never been obscured and may be said to be immediately
evident; the secondary and remoter precepts become known
only as a result of closer study and may be temporarily
eclipsed. The great jurist J. J. Burlamaqui puts the matter
very satisfactorily: "All that can be said on this subject is
that the most general and most important maxims of the law
of nature are so clear and manifest, and have such a proportion to our ideas, and such an agreeableness to our nature,
that as soon as they are proposed to us, one instantly approves of them. Natural law is that which so necessarily
agrees with the nature and state of man, that without ob-
serving its maxims, the peace and happiness of society can
never be preserved."[3]
Contrary to the Rationalists of the eighteenth and nine-
teenth centuries, we do not hold that the natural law is to
be derived from the abstract notion of man, but from the
observation of man in his historical setting. With the help
of experience we learn the germinal capacities of our nature
and the orientation which our activities must take in order
to realize the true human type. From such knowledge reason
formulates the natural law which guides nature toward the
term to which it spontaneously tends. "All those things,"
writes St. Thomas, "to which man has a natural inclination,
are naturally apprehended by reason as being good. Where-
fore according to the order of natural inclination is the order
of the precepts of the natural law."[4]
How ineradicably the natural law is etched on the human

[3] *The Principles of Natural and Political Law.*
[4] *Summa Theol.,* I, II, 94, 2.

heart may be deduced from the profound sense of duty very often to be observed in men of strong atheistic leanings. This shows the momentum of the innate impulse which carries rational nature to the acceptance of a supreme law.

5. POSITIVE LAW

Law is an ordinance of reason directed to the common good and promulgated by him who has authority over the community. The content of the law must come from reason; its form, the binding force, flows from the will of the legislator. The natural law cannot cover all details of human conduct and must be supplemented by positive legislation. The positive law, a rule of action, mandatory in form, freely established by competent authority, may be of divine or human origin. Its purpose is to specify the provisions of the natural law and apply them to particular conditions. It also attaches temporal sanctions to the decrees of the natural law in order to secure compliance from the recalcitrant members of the community. To be valid positive law must be in harmony with the natural law and violate no natural rights. Positive law derives its binding power from the natural law, since the latter inculcates respect for rightly constituted authority. Just civil laws, due to human enactment, therefore, bind in conscience; who disregards them is guilty of moral wrongdoing; the degree of the offense depends on the gravity of the matter involved. Certain laws, it is true, are merely penal, but to regard all civil legislation as of this type is an untenable assumption. Whilst regulations which are concerned only with the preservation of external order may be looked upon as merely penal, all statutes which aim at the prevention of public or private injury, or the safeguarding of rights, are invested with a genuinely binding authority. The special sphere of positive law is that vast field which the natural law leaves undetermined. To this sphere Leo XIII refers when he writes in the encyclical *Human Liberty:* "Now there are other enactments of the civil authority which do not follow directly, but somewhat remotely, from the natural law, and decide many points which the law of nature treats only in a general and indefinite way. It is in the constitution of these particular rules of life, suggested by reason and prudence, and put forth by competent authority, that human law, properly so called, consists, binding all citizens to work together for the attainment of the common end proposed to the community, and forbidding them to depart from this end."

The right attitude toward positive law is conditioned on the proper understanding of its benign purpose, which is not to annoy and subjugate men but to produce order, to promote harmonious social relations, to adjust rights and to make liberty possible for all. Those who are prone to look askance at legal regulations might profitably ponder that the law maps out the best way to peace and well-being, that it compels men to pursue their real interests and that, where it restrains, it is to curb the viciously inclined. Hence, positive law should be considered a helpful agency and elicit cheerful obedience. Liberty is possible only in a law-abiding nation, as Leo XIII remarks in the above-quoted encyclical: "It is an absolutely certain duty to respect authority and obey just laws; thus the citizen finds in the efficacy and vigilance of the law, aid and protection against the violence of the wicked."

6. THOU SHALT NOT!

Some pretend to take umbrage at the negative form in which moral precepts are frequently put, notably in the Decalogue. If, it is claimed, morality is in conformity with human nature, why does it abound with prohibitions and restrictions? Admitting that from the psychological and pedagogical point of view the excessive multiplication of negative precepts is not advisable and will make life appear unduly cramped and narrowed, it must, on the other hand, be maintained that it is often more effective to forbid the

evil which is to be avoided than to command the good which
is to be done. A prohibition can be cast into a very pregnant
form which gives sharper outline to a situation. Warning
signals to keep men away from danger are indispensable. It
will not do to leave a precipice without a notice strictly forbidding approach to the brink. But the prohibition is for
the sake of a positive good. Thou shalt not commit adultery,
on its positive side protects the sacredness of the home,
marital chastity and fidelity, the purity of love, and the dignity of the human sex relation. The "thou shalt not" fences
off an abyss lying along the road.

7. MORAL DEORDINATION AS SIN

We have not sounded the depth of moral iniquity until
we have recognized it as sin, that is, until we have seen it in
its radical opposition to God.

Since God commands the observance of the right order,
any deviation from this order takes on the character of an
offense against God. It becomes sin. Only when viewed
under this aspect, is moral evil understood in its real hei-
nousness. Because the world has lost the sense of sin, it takes
moral wrongdoing lightly. The element of sin is inseparable
from any violation of the moral order. To offend reason is
also to offend the God of reason. Duty, in its full sense, is
what must be done under pain of sin.

There is no satisfactory accounting for the absolute character of moral obligation without falling back on God as
the Author of the moral law, the supreme Legislator. Moral
evil is opposed to the Divine: to the Divine Essence, because
the moral law is the expression of the Divine Nature and
partakes of its holiness; to the Divine Will, because on account of his essential holiness God cannot but will the realization of the moral order by his creatures. Moral evil consists in the revolt of the personal will of man against the
sovereignty of God under which he was constituted to live.
The chief constituent of its malice is contempt for the su-

preme Ruler. As a violation of the harmony of the universal order, sin appears as a discordant element in this world and brings after it a train of physical, mental, and social evils. It is a terrible and tragic fact, the disruptive and ravaging influence of which is sadly manifest in human experience. As contempt of the will of God, sin brings on man Divine disfavor.

The concept of sin cannot be relegated to theology but has its rightful place in an ethical treatise, because it expresses an aspect of rational truth. We meet it, though in a mutilated form, in the text compiled by Drs. John Dewey and James H. Tufts, who will not be suspected of an undue religious bias. They write: "Sin is a significant ethical conception. It brings out the point that evil and wrongdoing are not merely individual matters, not merely failures; they offend against a law which is above the private self, against a moral order which has its rightful demands upon us."[5]

In its final analysis, then, moral obligation is the necessity of obeying the moral law under penalty of incurring the Divine displeasure, defying the holy and irresistible will of the Eternal and failing in the supreme purpose of existence.

8. THE AUTONOMY OF REASON

This phrase, playing an important part in Kant's system of morality, means that the supreme legislative authority is lodged in reason to which man owes absolute reverence and obedience. The source of duty accordingly would be in man himself who imposes the law on his own will without any reference to a superior will.

Kant's theory rests on a fallacy and is replete with contradictions. Man is not his own law nor his own independent legislator. Reason does not constitute the law but promulgates the law imposed by a higher power. The will cannot obligate itself, for this would make it debtor and creditor at the same time, subject and ruler in one person. If the law is

---

[5] *Ethics*, p. 104.

the product of man's own mind, it can neither have objective validity nor inspire him with that awe which Kant himself describes and which is universally felt by mankind.

XII

The Moral Sanctions

1. LOGIC OF MORAL SANCTIONS

In the moral world the law of causality holds the same sway as in the other realms of the universe. Everywhere compliance with the pertinent laws makes for good, disregard results in harm. The moral order is established for the good of man and embodies the rules of action consonant with his nature and, as a consequence, conducive to his perfection and happiness. In this order, means are solidly linked to ends and this connection cannot be broken. The end of the order cannot be had without the faithful use of the appropriate means, but fidelity to the order must infallibly secure the end. Refusal to submit to the order will entail forfeiture of the end.

This reasoning presupposes, however, that the moral order cannot be hampered and thwarted by any external interference. Now, if instead of taking a partial and fragmentary view of human life, confined to time, we look at it as embracing eternity, we can boldly assert that the moral order cannot be frustrated because it includes God as its source and guarantee. Infallibly moral goodness brings happiness, though it may be postponed. On the other hand, whoever rebels against the order cannot expect to share in its benefits and incurs the loss of the end which is happiness. Moral sanctions, therefore, that is happiness for the virtuous and unhappiness for the wicked, are based on sound reason.

They are not extrinsic and unrelated to morality but of its very essence. Happiness is the flowering of goodness; unhappiness the inevitable outgrowth of evil because morality is the way to happiness. The attainment of this end by fidelity to the moral order may be regarded as a natural result of our actions or as a Divine reward, and in the same manner the loss of happiness by disloyalty may be set down as a natural consequence or as a Divine punishment, since God as the Head of the moral order vindicates its rights and safeguards the interests of the just. St. Thomas very succinctly explains the nature of moral sanctions: "Wherever there exists a well-regulated order of ends it is necessary that this established order lead to an end; anything which separates itself from that order at the same time separates itself from its end. God has ordained a certain order for human acts in as far as their end is concerned, and this end is happiness. It follows, therefore, assuming this order to be solidly established that those who follow its dictates will obtain their end, happiness; in other words, they will be rewarded; and those who disturb this order by the commission of sin will not obtain their end, happiness; in other words, they will be punished."[1]

2. MERIT

Merit, the concomitant of every good act, is the acquisition of moral worth which confers a title or right to happiness. The title is effective with regard to God who is the supreme Ruler of the universe and the guarantor of the moral order. If merit did not attain to its object, justice would be frustrated. Merit is based on an inherent moral exigency and fitness which demand that a free act redound to the benefit of the agent. Morality, being so essentially a personal matter, must produce results, first of all, in terms of the individual. Hence, the good act must bring the agent immediate reward or a claim to a future reward. The good deed contains the seed of happiness which, however, does

[1] *Contra Gent.*, III, 140.

not always come to full fruitage in this life. It might also be said that merit resembles a surety bond which shall certainly be redeemed as its full value, unless canceled by the holder himself through mortal sin. By demerit, which is attendant on every evil act, moral unworth is incurred and the right to happiness forfeited. Demerit is not a constituent of guilt but consequent thereon. Just as the good action germinally contains happiness because it links the agent to his proper end, so the evil action, by which the agent is averted from his ultimate end and separated from the source of happiness, germinally contains misery.

3. LAW AND SANCTION

A sanction is a reward or penalty attached to observance or nonobservance of the law respectively. By means of its sanction the law is made effective. A lawgiver not backing his ordinances by appropriate sanctions would create the impression that he is not interested in their observance. The sanction must be proportioned to the disadvantages connected with the observance of the law and capable of compensating for any sacrifices made. Sanction reinforces the respect for duty and accordingly furnishes an added motive for law observance. It is really a help and intended to deter us from a course leading to disaster. So while rewards and punishments do not constitute, they do enforce duty and give it personal relevance. Education must have recourse to them and use them judiciously. Life is the education of man, and, therefore, likewise requires them.

The sanctions of the positive law are many and frequently arbitrary. The sanction of the natural law is essentially one and in accord with the very purpose of the moral order; attainment of the end for the good, and failure to attain the end for the evil. The end of man does not lie in the direction in which the immoral seek it and, consequently, will be missed. If man deliberately, persistently, and perversely continues on the wrong road, he cannot expect to reach the goal set for him and identified with his supreme happiness. He prepares for himself a state of misery. Cardinal D. Mercier brings out the inescapable logic of the situation, when he writes: "Man who finishes his time of probation obdurate in evil must be deprived of his end. This deprivation, which in Christian language we call damnation, excludes happiness."[2] It is a loss induced by man himself. A state of probation cannot go on indefinitely for thereby it would become meaningless; hence, finality must attach to the sanctions of the moral order. If there were no finality the moral law could not maintain its absolute supremacy. It stands to reason that this terrible lot will fall only on him whose will unto the last moment is obstinately set on evil and who passes into the world of fulfillment unrepentant and unregenerate. Such a condition of confirmed malice is mostly the result of habitual wrongdoing which gradually hardens the will in a definite mold.

4. NECESSITY OF SANCTIONS

Sanctions are inducements to observe the law and deterrents from violating it. They are indispensable for the very fact that man is a self and cannot disregard his own good.

The necessity of sanctions is objective and subjective. Objectively sanctions are demanded by justice. Without them the moral order would crumble and an intolerable state of general disorder and demoralization would follow, in which the unjust would enjoy an advantage over the just. If there were no sanctions the rights of merit would not be honored and the evildoer would be encouraged in his defiance of the law. Virtue unrewarded and vice unpunished strike us as an unbearable contradiction. The practice of virtue involves sacrifice and self-denial; these call for due recognition. Vice means self-gratification at the expense of the right order; such contempt for the law and the good of others cannot go unrebuked. Justice must balance the scales and restore the

[2] *La Psychologie*, p. 361.

disturbed order. The idea that there must be some satisfaction for order violated is deeply implanted in the moral consciousness of man.

Subjectively sanctions are required on account of human
frailty. They constitute a support against the vacillations of
the will and are a valuable auxiliary in the pursuit of duty.
For many the sanctions supply the ordinary motives for the
performance of duty. In proper appreciation of this fact
Gaston Sortais, S.J., writes in his *Treatise on Philosophy:*
"The sanction is not substituted for duty but added to it. It
comes to the assistance of the faltering will and strengthens
it in its fidelity to duty." Well-ordered self-regard is in itself
moral and may rightly figure as a legitimate motive in the
pursuit of the good. It does not at all deserve the scorn with
which some affect to look upon it.

5. INSUFFICIENCY   OF   TEMPORAL
SANCTIONS

Man's actions sometimes have disagreeable natural consequences which recoil on the doer. Utilitarianism holds that
these natural consequences of our actions are adequate sanctions of morality and sufficient to ensure moral conduct.
This is only partially true. If it may be admitted that very
often the transgressor brings upon himself severe chastise-
ment, it is also obvious that many a violator of the law entirely escapes the evil consequences of his sins. Many continue to enjoy the fruits of their injustice to the last breath
and seem to be favorites of fortune. The world is full of mis-
carriages of justice not merely in a legal, but in the higher
moral sense. Accounts are not settled in this life and moral
order remains unbalanced and unfavorable to the good and
partial to the wrongdoer. For if vice and crime do rarely in
this world meet with a full measure of retribution, it is even
more manifest that virtue hardly ever is rewarded according
to its deserts. The very nature of virtue places the conscientious at a disadvantage in this world, in which but too often

the honest become the victims of the unscrupulous. Melodrama would have us believe that innocence is always res-
cued from the clutches of villainy in the nick of time but
melodrama is not a true transcript of life, which more often
is stark tragedy. On the whole, we must conclude that if
there is no higher tribunal to set things right, moral goodness finds scant encouragement. The natural consequences of
wrongdoing fail to act as effective deterrents, and the temporal rewards of virtue prove but weak incentives to right
living. Social sanction is of no more avail for there are many
forms of immorality of which civil law takes no cognizance
and besides it is a notorious fact that social justice may be
readily outwitted.

That appeal to the natural consequences of immorality
will have but slight effect with the uneducated goes without
saying, but does knowledge of consequences prove a very
powerful restraint upon passion among the educated classes?
Our daily papers featuring the scandals in the higher brack-
ets of society answer that question in the negative. Patently
the dread of the temporal consequences of their misdeeds has
but slight effect on the fraudulent financier, the embezzling
bank director, the clever forger and the corrupt politician,
who not unfrequently figure in our criminal courts; yet the
native sagacity and the training which criminals of this type
invariably enjoy might have made them aware of the risks
they were running. In fact, knowledge of the injurious consequences attendant on immorality very often merely stim-
ulates caution and counsels careful restraint in the pursuit
of vice; it may even be employed for the express purpose of
obviating the natural consequences of immorality, so that a
career of vice may be indulged in with a great measure of
safety and practical impunity.

To prove efficacious sanctions must be absolutely inevitable and inescapable; and that holds good only of the otherworldly sanctions. To believe in a witness of conduct whose
knowledge reaches not alone action, however secret it may

be, but even thought; in whose hands are rewards and punishments of the weightiest character, and from whose judgment there is no escape, alone can secure compliance with duty in all circumstances. Hence, by practically the entire race the ultimate sanctions of morality have been conceived as lying outside of earthly life. This is also the conviction of Kant who wrote in *Religion within the Limits of Reason:* "The view into an illimitable future of happiness or misery is sufficient to serve as a motive to the virtuous to continue steadfast in well doing, and to arouse in the vicious the condemning voice of conscience to check his evil course."

Experience warrants the conclusion that the temporal rewards for moral effort are insufficient. That is particularly true when there is question of virtue that rises above the ordinary and assumes heroic proportions. Prudential considerations will not for long keep a man on the path of duty. It is palpably untrue that, as far as this world goes, virtuous living is invariably conducive to happiness. At best the utilitarian calculus would counsel restraint in vice but likewise great moderation in virtue. After all, only the grosser forms of vice prove seriously injurious to health or harmful to reputation. Society, as daily experience proves, is quite satisfied with a very low degree of morality and offers but slight encouragement to moral idealism.

6. THE   MORAL   COMPLEXION   OF   LIFE

Though the complete coincidence of moral goodness and happiness is not achieved in this earthly life, there is ample indication that such a consummation is preparing itself and that the good are on the way to this glorious goal. Generally it is true that the virtuous enjoy a greater measure of happiness than the wicked. It is this experience that gives some plausibility to the utilitarian argument. The grosser forms of vice often wreak a vengeance that is terrifying. Unbridled passion becomes an unbearable tyranny. Lack of discipline has wrecked many a promising career. Domestic peace is

ruined by selfishness. Poverty follows in the wake of extrava-
gance and dishonesty is often stripped of its ill-gotten gains.
By and large, the just, the honest, the benevolent, the industrious, the charitable, the law-abiding fare better than the
lawless. This holds even if we express happiness in material
terms. If we take higher ground and introduce such imponderable factors as peace of mind, serenity of conscience,
approval of the good, inner imperturbability, calm self-possession, freedom from fear, and joyous hopefulness, the balance
is all in favor of virtue. The tranquillity of a virtuous mind
is the highest form of happiness attainable in this life and
will reasonably be preferred to all material advantages. Confidently it may be asserted that the general pattern of man's
earthly existence reveals a distinctly moral design. What we
observe in this world lets us anticipate a full justice in the
next. Experience does not warrant moral pessimism.

7.   THE   OTHERWORLDLY   SANCTIONS

Morality becomes of overwhelming importance when it is
linked to eternal consequences. Even the glamour of sensual
attraction is dimmed when looked at in the light of an alternative of bliss or woe in a world to come. To seek momentary
satisfaction in preference to lasting happiness is a choice
which reason brands as folly. Nothing but the firm conviction that an endless hereafter awaits us after this time of trial
can account for the inextinguishable aspirations of our
higher self after good and happiness and give our will the
strength necessary to resist the cravings of the lower appetites. Even if we reduced morality to a prudential calcula-
tion, which most assuredly it is not, the prospect of otherworldly sanctions would supply impelling incentives for
right conduct and offer adequate compensation for whatever
sacrifices and renunciations a life of duty may exact. Against
the background of eternity the promises of this world pale
into utter insignificance and lose their glamour. Infinite
punishment and infinite reward administered by a judge

who can neither be deceived nor bribed offer interested motives that cannot be offset by any other consideration of self-interest. It would be nothing less than sheer madness to purchase momentary enjoyment at the price of enduring misery and suffering or to refuse quickly passing hardship that will be converted into an overflowing measure of endless bliss. Time has no equivalent for what eternity can give either in the way of reward or punishment. This, of course, represents an egotistical distortion and a mercenary construction of theistic ethics but even if we put the matter on this low basis the otherworldly sanctions enjoy an incontestable superiority over all other conceivable motives.

8. CONFLICT OF DUTY AND HAPPINESS

There is a form of moral pessimism which loves to dwell on the perennial conflict between duty and happiness, exaggerates the hardships of moral striving and paints the life of the virtuous on this side of the grave in the darkest colors. The life of the good is made to appear as a dreary, uneventful, tedious, and cheerless affair. The faint rays from the next world may bring a little light into it but cannot relieve its essential gloom. At best it is a life of dull resignation and weary waiting.

This picture is entirely out of focus. The life of moral endeavor and devotion to duty is in reality a life of high adventure, of magnificent courage, of splendid victories, of rich growth, of significant activity, of fine daring, and of profound spiritual satisfaction. There are high lights in it and stirring moments. It is not pure renunciation nor tedious boredom. The very virtue of fortitude which is indispensable to the man of duty implies that the virtuous life is a challenge and bears a martial character. Compared to it a life of self-indulgence is flat, uninspiring, and cowardly. True, in the beginning it makes heavy demands, but each conquest prepares for new conquests and fills us with the warm glow of a battle won. As progress is made, the path of virtue becomes less rugged and steep, and delights with the prospect of loftier heights. The moral life seems austere and forbidding only to the novice, but to face difficulties and wrestle with them in itself is joy.

The evolutionary ethics of H. Spencer is based on this very experience that morality, if consistently practiced, becomes more and more congenial and that our inclinations become progressively attuned to its requirements. Rightly he says: "The observation is not infrequent that persistence in performing a duty ends in making it a pleasure."[3] The practice of benevolence pays generous dividends in happiness as we are told in the Acts: "It is a more blessed thing to give rather than to receive" (20:35). Dr. Frank Thilly is unquestionably right when he remarks: "Life is not a continuous conflict between our inclinations, desires or impulses, and the sense of duty. . . . The 'thou shalt' is superseded by the 'I will,' and the rule of law gives way to the rule of love."[4] At many points duty and inclination converge. On the whole, the life of the man of duty is a pleasant one. Stolen pleasures are not always the sweetest but very often turn into wormwood. The life of duty gradually takes on a joyous spontaneity and blossoms into a freedom from which the element of coercion is almost completely absent. Let no one, therefore, be discouraged by the severe mien of duty when it first confronts him; as he becomes better acquainted with it, it will ingratiate and endear itself.

[3] *Data of Ethics*, p. 152.
[4] *Introduction to Ethics*, p. 110.

XIII

The Moral Character

1. THE MORAL PERSONALITY

The good deed itself passes away but it leaves an imprint on the doer and helps to shape his moral personality. Whatever man is doing, he is always making himself. Thus Aristotle says: "Man becomes righteous by performing righteous deeds and just by doing acts of justice."[1] Therein consists the abiding effect of every good action that to that extent it makes man good. Morality is something not merely to do but to become and to be. Progressively, by his acts man is moralized and his will fixed in the right direction. The moral law is wrought into his nature so that the good act becomes the expression of his character. The aim, therefore, of morality is to make man a moral personality steadfastly oriented toward the good. So merit is not an external title but a true quality of the self; it is recorded in the character of the individual. And character values are permanent because they are the actualized potentialities for good which lie unfinished in man and are brought to fruition by appropriate acts. We do not take our good deeds with us into the next life but we do take with us our moral personality which is the result of these deeds and which decides where we belong. To be good is the thing. Now God is good and holy by his innermost essence; man who has the capacity for good becomes good by doing good. Nor is this acquired

[1] *Op. cit.*, II, 1.

goodness a mere vesture in which man wraps himself, but a quality entering into his nature, intrinsically perfecting and transforming it.

The practice of morality, then, makes man a moral personality and thus prepares him for the eternal fellowship with the supreme Spirit, who, holy by nature, gathers around him those who have become holy by their works. Man must achieve sanctity as an inner personal quality to be a worthy member of this blessed community. He can be a citizen of the City of God only if he fits himself for this holy citizenship by acquiring that internal conformity to righteousness which is the law of this perfect community. To enter into this society of moral selves, which is not ruled by restraint, his will must be in basical harmony with the moral order and his entire being in tune with holiness. Such a disposition is the outcome of the practice of virtue by which the good becomes natural to us. That, then, is the ultimate significance of virtue. But virtue also has the more immediate purpose of assisting us in this time of approbation because in the ordinary course of events our final destiny for better or worse is not settled by one act but by repeated acts.

2. THE VIRTUOUS MAN

The good man is not he who occasionally performs a good act but rather he whose conduct manifests a uniform tendency toward the good and who practices what is right with constancy and consistency. Such a man we call a virtuous man. To him right conduct has become a second nature which enables him to fulfill his duties with spontaneous ease and with true delight. Such a happy condition must be acquired and is the fruit of persistent moral striving. It consists in habits which impart to the faculties a fixed direction toward the good, and a dynamic inclination toward its practice. The virtuous man no longer lives on the level of impulsive tendencies but on the higher plane of volitional choices which have solidified into stable modes of conduct. He has passed the stage where moral decisions involve severe struggles and call for considerable effort.

3. VIRTUES AND VICES

The distinction exists in every language and always amounts to this that the virtues are those habitual forms of conduct which realize the conception of the better and nobler self, whilst the vices designate personality traits which do not befit a noble character and, carrying with them the notion of stain and defilement, mar and depreciate human selfhood. The vicious man is less worthy to be called a man.

A man only then deserves to be called virtuous when he possesses all the virtues required by his state of life, at least in a germinal condition. This would seem exacting if there did not exist a close interrelation between the various virtues so that the one drew after itself the others. Accordingly, the virtuous man makes the impression of well-balanced development, of all-round perfection, and of moral symmetry. The virtues correspond to the various aspects of objective goodness and to our different duties, and as there is a fundamental unity in goodness so there is an essential correlation between the virtues. The man who engages earnestly in the striving for goodness tends to develop all the virtues harmoniously.

Virtues are necessary because without them we would be obliged in every recurring moral situation to make again a new deliberate choice which would call for much effort and render the practice of the good arduous and discouraging.

The moral life should also be governed by the principle of economy which means that it be reduced to a system of habits devised to cope with the ordinary situations of everyday existence and to save in such recurring cases the labor incident on a deliberate choice. Life is not made up of unrelated, disconnected situations, and hence, neither is moral conduct a series of isolated choices but rather a matter of fixed attitudes. The moral life becomes an organic structure in which minor choices are integrated with more comprehensive ends which in their turn are subordinated to a supreme purpose. The mature moral man has definitely chosen a course which he pursues and does not at every crossroad debate with himself in which direction he shall turn. He does not everlastingly fight the same battles over again and certain moral issues as far as he is concerned are definitely settled once for all.

Today contains tomorrow. A choice made at this moment will influence future choices. A particularly decisive choice made now may determine the course of my conduct for a long time to come. Choices are seeds which develop and bear fruit in the days and years that follow. There are critical moments in life when both good and evil are set before us and when we implicitly embrace an upward or downward leading course. We carry the past with us and it either weighs us down or buoys us up.

Virtue is a habit perfecting the rational faculty and inclining it toward the good. It can affect only those faculties which are subject to volitional control. It is built up by repeated acts. The intellectual virtues prompt the right choice, the moral virtues make it easy to carry out what has been recognized as good. Since it is possible for man to act against his better judgment, intellectual virtues are not enough, especially in sudden onrushes of passion only habits or moral discipline can provide safety. Whereas the intellectual virtues come by study, the moral virtues can only be reaped as the result of eternal vigilance, prolonged discipline, and determined resistance to the allurements of sensuality. They are the reward given to man for repeated conquests of self.

As virtue consists in due proportion and right measure, a virtue can turn into its opposite either by excess or defect. Since virtue embodies the idea of measure, and measure is a rational concept, it readily appears that the virtuous man has brought all his inclinations under the domination of reason. By discipline measure can be wrought into the appetites which lack an inherent regulative principle.

4. THE GROUNDWORK OF VIRTUES

There are certain pivotal virtues on which the whole moral life turns and which regulate all human relations. They are called cardinal virtues and are four in number. Their function is to establish the right order between man's reason and his sensual nature and between man and his fellow men. Prudence enables man readily to discern what is the proper thing to do in given circumstances. Temperance rules the feelings and the irrational appetite. It is synonymous with self-control and extends to all forms of impulsive life. When great hindrances arise in the pursuit of the good fortitude or courage is necessary to surmount these obstacles. Courage is the moral power to overcome the natural fear of pain and danger when a moral good is at stake. It takes its inspiration from the conviction that there are better things than life and evils worse than death. A measure of heroism is indispensable in every life. All are called on to practice fortitude in its less spectacular manifestations such as patience, perseverance, and constancy. Serenity and calmness of mind also belong to fortitude because it is often difficult to maintain inner tranquillity under severe provocation. Justice, which will be dealt with more fully, puts us in the right relation to our fellow men.

5. THE VIRTUOUS CHARACTER

Character marks the highest point of moral attainment. It rises superior to the level of impulsive action and, accordingly, represents many triumphs over the instinctive tendencies of sensual nature. Where we have character, will is the controlling factor and life is dominated by principles. This, as we know but too well, is a culminating achievement resulting from many battles with the influences that dispute the supremacy of the will. The most devastating thing that can be said about an individual is that he has no character. Such individuals are the despair of the educator because of their flabbiness. Only good material can be sculptured into a lasting form. Persons referred to are of a pulpy nature that will not take an edge; it runs easily into any mold but will not keep shape.

The self is originally plastic but, if of the real stuff, will gradually harden into a definite cast and hold its form. Character, thus, is not the equilibrium of diverse impulses but the mastery of the impulses by an internal principle of control. It betokens the unification of all tendencies into a consistent and coherent whole, expressive of a personal ideal and firmly knit into a harmonious structure of moral purposes. Stability is its outstanding attribute. It is forged by the will and cannot be formed by drifting comfortably and passively with the stream of life. The chief agency in the formation of character is self-education. Since human character can never reach absolute harmony and all-round perfection, it usually exhibits some dominant trait and stresses some particular aspect of moral goodness, from which it receives an individual complexion; thus, we speak of a just, a benevolent, a kindly, a submissive, a self-reliant character. The reason for this is that, whilst character is truly what we make ourselves, the final outcome depends on our native endowment from which it derives its coloring. No artist can surmount the essential limitations of his material and no man can be other than himself. Every man must aim at being the best self he can be. If he tries to put on a character which is not rooted in his natural abilities the result will not be character but a farcical impersonation, a ludicrous mask, a ridiculous pose.

Summing up we may say that character is a graft that improves and transforms nature. Nature is the raw material of moral life, rich in unrealized potentialities; it is the undisciplined, unmoralized, and unsocialized man. Character, the fruit of incessant toil, stands for the disciplined, moralized, and socialized man. The road from nature to character is long and arduous but it leads to that higher freedom in which will and law coincide and duty becomes a joyous performance.

XIV

Rights and Justice

1. THE SUBJECT OF RIGHTS

A right is a moral power to do, to hold or to exact something. By his rights man is protected against undue interference from others. His dignity and liberty are safeguarded and he is assured that measure of self-determination which is required by a rational being. His rights are exceedingly precious to man and he is naturally jealous of them.

Man is the bearer of rights because he possesses the attribute of personality. Personality roots in self-consciousness and implies control over one's own actions. Only in virtue of self-consciousness can I refer a thing to myself and claim it as mine. Only he who can say I, can say mine. A person is his own and exists and acts for himself; a person is autocentric and cannot be made a means. A thing is not for its own sake; it is subordinated to the use of a person by whom it may be owned and who may make it serve his own advantage. Man is never a thing and chattel, neither in relation to other men nor to society and the State. Man is *sui juris* and entitled to live his own life, and fashion it along the lines of a rational choice.

Man has rights because he has an end for the attainment of which he is responsible. No power may intervene between him and his destiny and prevent him from doing what is necessary for the realization of his end. My right connotes in all others the duty to respect this right. A right is something sacred and its violation means the violation of human personality. One of the chief purposes of organized government is the protection of rights. To do this a state employs its restraining and coercive power. Might must serve right. Not all rights, however, can be exacted by the application of physical force; they are true rights notwithstanding and morally inviolable. A moral right which is recognized and enforced by the State becomes also a legal or juridical right. Inalienable rights are those without which man cannot work out his ultimate end.

Man's rights are rooted in his duty toward God who has established for him an end from which he may not be averted. From his relationship to God flow man's independence and freedom. If God is his supreme master, he cannot have another supreme master; if he belongs primarily to God, he cannot completely belong to another, not even to himself. He has relations to others but these are overshadowed by his relation to God, to which he appeals against oppression. Hence Pius XII writes: "Christian teaching alone, in its majestic integrity, can give full meaning and compelling motive to the demand for human rights and liberties, because it alone gives worth and dignity to human personality. In consequence of his high conception of the nature and gifts of man, the Catholic is necessarily the champion of true human rights and the defender of true human liberties; it is in the name of God Himself that he cries out against any civil philosophy which would degrade man to the position of a soulless pawn in a sordid game of power and prestige."[1]

2. NATURAL RIGHTS

Some fundamental rights belong to man by reason of his very nature. These rights are prior to civil law, which, as a consequence, must respect them and is limited by them. It is the principal aim of society to protect individuals in the

[1] *The Ecclesiastical Review*, Jan. 1939.

enjoyment of these natural rights which are vested in them by the immutable laws of nature. The State may not abrogate them but is bound to uphold and enforce them as far as it can. Their exercise may be regulated in conformity with the exigencies of society but they cannot be sacrificed to social or political expediency.

Whilst it is true that the State can create and confer certain rights, it would be false to assert that the State is the ultimate and exclusive source of all rights. If all rights were created by the State, they could also be canceled by the same authority and no manner of treatment of the citizens would be unjust; the State would have no duties toward individuals and could deal with them as things and chattels.

The obvious fact, however, is that the individual as well as the family exist antecedently to the State and, having being independently of the State, they likewise possess by natural endowment the right to all things necessary for their proper existence and development.

Every other theory legitimizes tyranny, despotism, and oppression. Thus W. C. Robinson writes in *Elements of American Jurisprudence*: "Were it true that all of our rights are derived from the State, not only would there be no obligation to obey public authority, but the State, when formed, or the ruling majority in it, would possess absolute dominion over the persons and property of its citizens, and however unjust and unreasonable its acts might be, they could work no wrong to anyone, since wrong consists in the violation of rights and there could be no rights except such as the State, or the majority in it, might see fit to concede." Hence, the denial of natural rights contains the most sinister implications.

The basic law of our country accepts the theory of natural rights when it solemnly declares: "We hold these truths to be self-evident: that all men are created equal; that they are endowed by their Creator with certain inalienable rights; that among these are life, liberty, and the pursuit of happi-

ness." This view which makes rights the expression and natural prerogative of personality and the State the custodian
and interpreter of these rights is the bulwark of true liberty
and the only basis of sound legislation. Where this view is
held, the positive law embodies, formulates, and protects
the rights of man and thus becomes a true version of the
natural law. The Pastoral Letter of the American Hierarchy
of September, 1919, amplifies this idea: "In the light of this
central truth, we can understand and appreciate the principle on which our American liberties are founded — 'that
all men are endowed by their Creator with certain inalienable rights.' These are conferred by God with equal bounty
upon every human being, and therefore, in respect of life,
liberty, and the pursuit of happiness, the same rights belong
to all men and for the same reason. Not by mutual conces-
sion or covenant, not by warrant or grant from the State, are
these rights established; they are the gift and bestowal of
God. In consequence of this endowment, and therefore in
obedience to the Creator's will, each of us is bound to respect
the rights of his fellow men. This is the essential meaning
of justice, the great law antecedent to all human enactment
and contrivance, the only foundation on which may rest
securely the fabric of society and the structure of our political, legal, and economic systems."

3. ANIMALS ARE NOT ENDOWED WITH RIGHTS

This in no way justifies wanton cruelty. Man may use
animals for his needs according to the intentions of the
Creator which does not imply that he may inflict unnecessary suffering on them. Who delights in torturing helpless
animals brutalizes his own nature and stifles the sentiment
of sympathy in his own breast. On the other hand, a mawk-
ish sentimentality in regard to animals may render one cal-
lous toward one's fellow men. "Is it not a fact," asks Father
John Gerard, S.J., "that many who expend their sympathy

upon cats and dogs have but little left for the poor; that they are not remarkable for their kindness and consideration toward their dependents; that sometimes even their own children appear to hold a lower place in their hearts than do their pets?"[2] Children should be trained to treat animals kindly in order to accustom them to considerate regard for their fellow men. If a tendency to cruelty is noticed it should be speedily checked.

4. BASIC NATURAL RIGHTS

A. The Right to life and bodily integrity is consequent on the very fact of existence. Logically it includes the right to self-defense. It likewise entitles to the things necessary for the maintenance of life. Unless forfeited by crime, human life may not be taken by any earthly authority nor may any mutilation be inflicted except as a penalty for a crime committed. Since life and the body are from God and intended for a purpose, they do not absolutely belong to man and hence suicide and self-mutilation are also unlawful. The right to life extends to prenatal existence. From the preceding it follows that euthanasia (mercy killing) and eugenical sterilization are contrary to the moral law. Indirect killing, if not intended as a means but inevitably following from an act good in itself, may be permitted. Respect for the sacredness of life is essential to human wellbeing and civilization.

B. The Right of the freedom of conscience consists in the immunity from external compulsion in following outwardly the dictates of conscience. To this category belongs the right of religious freedom. Men have held this right sacred and have been willing to suffer for their convictions. St. Peter asserted this right when he told the Sanhedrin: "We ought to obey God rather than men" (Acts 5:29). Conscience is a sanctuary which may not be invaded by any temporal authority. The practice of religion may not be impeded except

[2] Vaughan, J. T., *Thoughts for All Times*, p. 404.

in a case where an act conflicts with the rights of another or is socially injurious. No man may be forcibly made to embrace a religion. To the right of freedom of worship corresponds on the part of public authority the duty of religious tolerance. This in no wise sanctions religious indifferentism nor gives countenance to the claim that one religion is as good as another, but it recognizes the fact of invincible ignorance. For the affairs of his conscience man is responsible only to his Maker.

C. The Right of free speech which includes the freedom of the press and of instruction. Liberty of opinion is, of course, beyond external control but the expression of opinion is something else. Freedom of discussion is favorable to the progress of truth and constitutes a wholesome check on government. This freedom, however, cannot be allowed to degenerate into license which would corrupt morality or endanger social order and stability. The dissemination of improper literature should be duly checked and a reasonable censorship exercised over stage and screen. Against defamation and malicious libel there ought to be adequate legal redress. Freedom of speech cannot be invoked to cover insidious destructive propaganda which besmirches all that is sacred to mankind. Society infringes no right when it defends itself against subversive doctrines, against spiritual poisoning, against the overthrow of the foundations of civilization, against the dynamite which would blow up our religious, family, and social traditions and wreck the entire structure of the social order.

5. JUSTICE

Justice is respect for the rights of others. It regulates the relations between man and man and thus becomes the cornerstone of society. It enters into all human contacts and must be present wherever men live together. Its absence makes order, peace, and harmony impossible and would produce an intolerable state of mutual aggression, warfare, and utter social chaos. Aptly Aristotle says in his *Politics:* "For man when perfected is the best of animals, but when separated from law and justice, he is the worst of all. . . . But justice is the bond of men in states, and the administration of justice, which is the determination of what is just, is the principle of order in political society." When we consider that it is not restricted to property rights but extends to all rights, its pivotal character becomes apparent. The just man injures and harms no one. Rightly great encomiums have been heaped on this resplendent virtue. Cicero wrote in *De Officiis:* "In justice, on the basis of which men are called good, virtue shines forth most resplendently." Men instinctively resent unjust treatment and rebel against it. The innate sense of justice implanted in man is well described by Professor Walter Rauschenbusch who says: "We can gauge the ethical importance of justice by the sense of outrage with which we spontaneously react against injustice. Its permanent denial makes men hard and bitter. . . . Practically all the internal upheavals recorded in history were caused by the agonized attempts of inferior classes to resist or shake off the clutch of injustice. Nations die of legalized injustice. It is more deadly even than sexual vice or alcoholism."[3] Substantially in agreement with this is what the late President Harding said: "All of us demand liberty and justice. There cannot be one without the other, and they must be held the unquestioned possession of all peoples. Inherent rights are of God, and the tragedies of the world originate in their attempted denial."

6. NATURE OF JUSTICE

We define justice as the constant and permanent determination of the will to give to each one his due. It is not a sentimental affair dependent on moods, as generosity might be, but something to be measured by objective standards and

[3] Rauschenbusch, W., *Christianizing the Social Order*, Macmillan Co., N. Y., p. 333.

which is always urgent because what I owe my fellow men
clamors to be fulfilled. Debts of every kind have an imperious voice which refuses to be silenced. Justice excludes arbitrariness and measures with an unbending yardstick.
There is a clearness and precision about the duties of justice
which the requirements of other virtues lack. There is a
stern finality about justice, it must be accomplished. Years
do not obliterate the claims of justice. Injustice has incon-
venient, unescapable consequences: it calls for reparation
and restitution.

Justice asserts a certain basic equality among men. No
man, however high his position may be, is exempt from
duties of justice toward his fellow men who still remain his
equals in their essential nature. No one has only rights over
another one. Where men come into contact with one
another, rights and duties arise simultaneously on both sides.

7. DIVISIONS OF JUSTICE

Commutative justice answers to the definition of justice
in its fullest sense. It is only here that the strict obligation
of restitution applies and the full equalization of thing with
thing obtains. Commutative justice governs contracts and all
relations in which an exchange takes place. It is violated by
an injury done to another's property, bodily integrity, good
name, and family rights. Alienation of affection also constitutes such a violation.

Distributive justice obligates those who function as the
officials of public authority. Too often those in power imagine that they may distribute public burdens and favors as
they please. Violations of distributive justice are favoritism,
partiality, official negligence, oppression, and extortion. Such
violations produce public discontent and may in extreme
cases lead to revolution.

Legal justice is the enduring will of the citizen to give
civil authority its due. It is fulfilled by observance of the
laws of the realm. It is violated by infractions of the statutes,

shirking of social burdens, corruption of officials, and perjury. Legal equality is not an absolute one, but one of proportion. Considered precisely as men, all men are equal
before the law. Equal protection of the law is a guarantee
of social peace and governmental stability.

Social justice is concerned with the distribution of the
national wealth on the basis of the common good and in
conformity with fundamental human equality. Its chief
object is to regulate economic relations, among the most
outstanding of which are the wage contract and the just
price. It forbids us to treat labor as a mere commodity and
demands that the wage be determined with regard to the
needs of the laborer. No wage which is not a living wage can
be considered a just wage. Social justice binds those who own
the instruments of production, manage industry, and distribute the national income. It is the office of the State to
specify and enforce the demands of social justice by appropriate social legislation.

8. JUSTICE AND CHARITY

However important justice is in social life, men could not
possibly live together on a basis of mere justice. It truly
would make life too hard and too harsh. Justice, therefore,
requires charity as an essential supplement. Some ethicians
include benevolence and kindness in justice; it is well, however, to keep a clear line of demarcation between justice and
charity and not to confuse their respective spheres. Though
the two should be united, substitution of the one for the
other is not acceptable. I cannot absolve myself from duties
of justice by a more extended practice of charity. In justice
I give to my neighbor what is his; and that comes first. In
charity I give of my own. The latter is unquestionably
higher, if the former has been done. But if the former has
been neglected, the latter becomes arbitrariness and
hypocrisy.

The motivation of justice is the idea of equality, a somewhat frigid, almost mathematical notion; the inspiration of charity is the concept of human brotherhood, a heart-warming ideal. Naturally charity will prove a more generous soil on which fairer flowers will grow. Charity is expansive and urges us to be all things to all men; it prompts courtesy, cheerfulness, and good humor in social intercourse and suggests the chivalries and considerateness of friendship. It is plain that we owe a brother more than an equal but the claims of charity cannot be reduced to exact measurement and leave a wide margin for individual choice and sentiment. Emotion which may enter into charity has no place in justice. Justice adheres to strict measure and that is why its duties are clear cut and rigid, and determined by objective standards. So Dr. P. Wheelwright says: "Whatever else justice may connote, it implies at very least a stern objectivity. One cannot be just in an impulsive and irrational way."[4]

Inferior though justice, when compared to charity, may be, it must be accorded priority. Its precise demands have precedence over the vaguer claims of charity or benevolence. This, however, is not intended to sanction the flimsy cry, not charity but justice, for both are needed, withal in the right order. Untempered by benevolence, justice readily degenerates into a dangerous fanaticism. On the other hand, the sentimentalists are too prone to accept benevolence as a substitute for justice. Justice represents the steel framework, the structural element of society, to which much may be added but from which nothing can be taken away.

Justice is vitalized and rendered dynamic by charity. He who does not also cultivate charity, will soon fall short of justice. Accordingly Pius XI declares in *Quadragesimo Anno* that social justice cannot be effected without charity: "Now, in effecting this reform, charity must play a leading part. How completely deceived are those reformers who, zealous only for justice, proudly disdain the help of charity. Charity cannot take the place of justice unfairly withheld, but, even

[4] *Op. cit.*, p. 254.

though a state of things be pictured in which every man receives at least all that is due, a wide field will nevertheless remain open for charity. For justice alone, even though most faithfully observed, can remove indeed the cause of social strife, but can never bring about a union of hearts and minds."

9. RIGHTS AND DUTIES

Man has an instinctive sense of rights and this sense should be developed. Not to protest against injustice frequently indicates only a base spirit and a love of ease. A generation which is indifferent to its rights leaves posterity a baleful inheritance, for craven submission to unjust demands tends to increase the arrogance of those in power. There is something sacred about rights conferred by God, and men do wisely to be obstinate in their defense. There is nothing noble in slave mentality. Withal there are occasions when to surrender one's rights is the highest exercise of one's freedom. But if we cultivate a keen sense of our rights, it is even more essential to reinforce the sense of duty and responsibility. The man who always stands on his rights becomes unbearable. He is very likely to overstress his rights and to make unwarranted claims. The man devoted to duty ranks higher than the man overjealous of his rights. Right is the selfish, duty the generous, side of human relations. The passion for rights may arouse men to overthrow tyranny but it does not suffice to build up a well-ordered and harmonious community. The only constructive social principle is duty. In this sense Bishop J. L. Spalding wrote in *Glimpses of Truth:* "Accustom thyself to the thought that the rights are of minor importance, the fulfillment of thy duties being the essential thing." A sense of one's own dignity goes well with respect for the rights of others.

It is a serious pedagogical error to show no regard for the rights of children. Such treatment will breed sullen resentment and smoldering rebellion or produce a servile disposition and an unmanly submissiveness. Men of the latter type become the instruments of oppression in the hands of tyrants. He who has a high regard for rights as God-given instrumentalities will not allow himself to be used as a tool to defraud his fellow men of their rights.

10. VIRTUES RELATED TO JUSTICE

The following virtues are cognate to justice of which they represent particular aspects: religion, loyalty, respect, gratitude, obedience. truthfulness, faithfulness, friendship, equity, fairness, filial regard and love of country. Justice thus appears to be a root from which many excellent fruits grow.

PART II
Special Ethics

I

The Moral Life

This part of ethics deals with concrete and practical phases of the moral life. It contains the applications of the natural law to the basic relations in which man stands to the universal order and to which he must adjust himself in conformity with the requirements of reason. It gives definite form to man's rights and duties and shows how the moral life actually must be led. On this account it is called special or applied ethics.

The moral life presents two main aspects, the individual and the social. Hence we speak of individual and social ethics. Still the two spheres cannot be completely separated, but overlap at many points and have broad surfaces of contact. Man is a self, but a self essentially linked with other selves. No man lives to himself. Individual morality does not gain by being detached from social morality. Social relations are not imposed from without but center in man's very being. Social morality is not the morality of society but the morality of the individual in relation to society. The ethical unit is the person. Accordingly, the individual and social aspects of morality are unified in the concept of personal morality. This concept of the personal character and the real unity of the moral life forestalls that fatal dualism, so common in our days, which sets up one code of principles for the conducting of private affairs and a different one for the management of public affairs. Morality knows not the divided life. It is cut out of one cloth and throughout of identical texture. Man as an individual self and as a member of society is the same person. Honesty of man to man and honesty in business are of the same grain.

For the sake of convenience, however, we divide this section into individual and social ethics. The former is concerned with the proper conduct of man in reference to God, to himself and to his fellow men; the latter treats of man as a member of society and of the special rights and duties entailed by membership in a social unit.

II

Duties Toward God

1. GOD

From natural theology we take, not as postulates, but as
demonstrated conclusions certain truths relative to the
existence and attributes of the Divinity. We learn that God
exists, that he is a being of infinite perfection, that he is a
Personal Self and the Creator of the universe and of man,
that He knows and wills, that He has called this world into
being for a purpose and that His Providence directs all
things to their end. He is the supreme Lawgiver and His will
is the rule to which everything must conform. God's sovereignty is the necessary consequence of the fact of creation
and of the utter dependence of all created beings on Him.
He has established order both for His glory and the good of
creation and wills that this order be fulfilled. He is not indifferent to His creation but mindful of the work of His
hands. He loves His creatures and is good to them. Everything He guides to its final consummation. He is holy and
just.

Now man is also a personal self and the cosmic situation
described will naturally arouse in him an appropriate
response.

2. RELIGION

Man must accept this universe and his place in it; that
means that he must accept God and his relation to Him. The

conscious acceptance of his position involves for man a recognition of the sovereignty of God, an acknowledgment of the supreme authority of God, loyalty to the Ruler of the world, submission to the Divine Will, an avowal of his dependence on God's power, a confession of his own state of servant and willingness to serve, reverence for the Divine Majesty, gratitude toward God's goodness, love for his Maker, confidence in God as the Rewarder of the good and fear of God's judgments, respect for God's greatness, and some manifestation of these sentiments. That is man's attitude toward God which reason dictates when it considers the relation in which man stands with regard to God. All this is comprised in religion. Religion, then, is the personal, consciously accepted relation of the created self to the Creator. It is the voluntary and free acceptance of the inescapable physical bond which binds man to his Maker. Any other attitude contradicts the very facts of reality. It is God's absolute right to claim such voluntary subjection on the part of the rational creature. Hence we read in Deuteronomy: "What doth the Lord thy God require of thee, but that thou fear the Lord thy God, and walk in his ways, and love him, and serve the Lord thy God, with all thy heart and with all thy soul?" (10:10.) Religion, thus, is nothing more than a free recognition of objective, incontrovertible facts.

3. DEFINITION OF RELIGION

Religion is a moral virtue which disposes us to render to God the complete allegiance which is due to Him and in particular to offer Him the worship and homage to which His supreme excellence entitles Him. Respect is the tribute which we pay to moral grandeur before which our mind bows in spontaneous recognition of superior worth and dignity. In the presence of the holiness and august position of God this respect is elevated and intensified to worship and adoration. To deny religious homage to God, the splendor of whose glory fills the universe and on whose earth we mortals live, bespeaks an incredible indifference to the highest values and argues an intolerable insolence. Moreover, it is not enough to say with Kant that religion consists wholly in the observance of the moral law; of course, obedience to the moral law is the duty of man but besides that he owes God the explicit expression of deference and veneration.

Like morality, religion is a universal phenomenon. It first begins with man's realization of his dependence on a being superior to himself, a being who inspires him with reverence and awe, who avenges wrongdoing, from whom he may obtain succor and to whom he feels compelled to render external worship. Though fear predominates in the more imperfect forms of divine worship, it can neither be regarded as the source nor the exclusive element of religion for man looks to the superior powers he worships for protection against the destructive forces of nature and the malevolent designs of evil beings. As the idea of the fatherhood of the supreme Being supersedes that of an exacting and relentless Deity, fear passes into filial reverence and is more and more replaced by trust and love.

Primarily religion is an attitude of the will and as such presupposes an intellectual factor, but because it bears on issues of paramount importance, it involves also a strong emotional resonance. It embraces the whole man, his reason, his volition, and his affective side. In the genesis of religion, intellectual apprehension precedes, and will action and passional response follow. Thus religion is neither pure sentiment nor mere cognition but a decision of the will based on rational grounds and involving far-reaching consequences capable of stirring feeling to its greatest depth. It embodies a declaration of loyalty to the supreme Ruler of the universe and an implicit promise of obedience to his law. Objectively we understand by religion a sum of truths expressing man's relations to God and the practical duties flowing from these relations. A religion is false when it wrongly states the nature of God, erroneously conceives the relation of man to God, and as a consequence errs with regard to the ways in which God is to be served and worshiped. Only religious practices based on the truth and in conformity with the holiness of God can be pleasing to the Creator.

Though it cannot be held that all religions are equally true and good, we should mutually respect each other's honest religious convictions and embrace in charity all men whatever religious creed they may profess.

Worship must be internal as well as external. This is required by the composite nature of man and the intimate relations between body and soul. External practices without the inward quickening spirit, that is, pure lip service, have no value; interior devotion without appropriate expression is likely to die of inanition as a fire without fuel. As man is a social being, social and public worship is also necessary. Common worship has special power to uplift the soul and to unite men in the consciousness of brotherhood. On this point Leo XIII writes in the encyclical *Immortale Dei:* "Nature and reason, which command every individual devoutly to worship God in holiness, because we belong to Him and must return to Him since from Him we came, bind also the civil community by a like law. For men living together in society are under the power of God not less than individuals are, and society, no less than individuals, owes gratitude to God, who gave it being and maintains it, and whose ever bounteous goodness enriches it with countless blessings. It is a public crime to act as though there were no God." The anarchism of our days and the class hatred which threatens to disrupt society to a large extent can be traced to the consistent neglect of public worship on the part of governments.

4. RELIGION A DUTY AND A NECESSITY

Man endowed with intellect and will and enjoying the privilege of self-determination must assume in the world and in respect to its author the place which right order demands; that means that he must freely submit to the dominion of God and honor Him who is the supreme Excellence and sovereign Good in a proper manner. Religion brings us into authentic relations with the Creator. To refuse religious worship would mean for man to assert his absolute independence and complete autonomy. So religion is embedded in the very structure of the cosmic scheme. If there is a God, He must be acknowledged, worshiped, and obeyed by His rational creatures. It is no valid objection to say that God does not need man's worship and does not benefit thereby. It is His right. He is worthy of such outward honor, as Holy Writ says: "Thou art worthy, O Lord our God, to receive glory and honor and power; because thou hast created all things, and for thy will they were, and have been created" (Apoc. 4:11).

Man needs religion. The union of man with God is the condition of man's fullest self-development and the attainment of his happiness. Religion satisfies man's deepest aspirations and raises him above what is earthly. Without it the world would be submerged in materialism and sink into the cult of the carnal. Cultural progress does not render religion superfluous since it retains its hold on ages of the most advanced civilization. There is not the slightest indication that man will outgrow the need of religion for it is not a temporary pedagogue during mankind's pupilage, to be dismissed when the pupil comes of age.

Orderly social life is possible only on a religious basis for religion secures respect for law and restrains the mighty since it makes human authority responsible to one higher.

The blessings of religion are many. It sustains man in the disappointments of life and is a source of solace in sorrow and bereavement. Without the religious outlook, the world would be a very inhospitable place for man and the horizon would close in on him like the gray walls of a huge prison from which there is no door opening into a better world.

Since only one religion can be true, it is incumbent on man honestly to go in search of this one true religion and not to satisfy himself with the shallow and insincere notion that it does not matter what religion we profess. It is especially the duty of every serious man to study the claims of revealed religion.

Both the tremendous personal importance and the social value of religion are strikingly described by Dr. Ladd: "Primarily religion is an affair of the individual soul. Its first and constantly repeated question is not, How do I stand toward society? but, How do I stand toward God? And this is a question which concerns everyone as though there were no other one in all the wide world. Of course, we do not mean that religion has nothing to do with social betterment and social reform; on the contrary, we believe that it always has been and always must be, the greatest of all the forces that operate to lift up the social condition and to promote the social welfare of mankind."[1]

5. PRAYER

Humanity has always lifted its voice to the powers that preside over the destinies of the world. Man's impotence has in all climes and at all times found articulate expression in humble supplications sent up to the heavens. Prayer is inseparable from religion. Without the practice of prayer religious sentiment atrophies as a plant dies when deprived of moisture. If God is truly a personal self then vocal communion between the human self and God becomes a very natural thing. Neglect of prayer leads to worldliness and to oblivion of the things of the spirit and eternity. In prayer God becomes a vivid reality to our consciousness. Well says Fechner: "Take prayer out of the world and it is as if you had cut the tie between humanity and God, silenced the tongue of the child in reference to its father." And A. Saba-

[1] Ladd, Dr. G., *What Ought I to Do?*, Longmans, Green and Co., N. Y., p. 281.

tier in like manner: "A religion without prayer leaves man and God in mutual remoteness with no intimate commerce, no interior communion, no interchange, no action of God in man, no return or response of man to God."[2] In prayer man seeks the Divine Fellowship and opens his soul to the sanctifying influences of the Divine Presence. This explains the invariable concomitants of prayer, calm, peace, confidence, and courage. Prayer dispels our fears and takes away the smart of anxiety for our daily needs. Its effect on the human mind is most beneficent. It purifies the soul and disciplines our desires. It is an unfailing fountain of moral energy and taps the deepest resources of the will. By its unifying influence on the whole personality it prevents internal conflicts and gives a uniform orientation to all our striving. In mental hygiene it plays an important part, as W. James writes: "The exercise of prayer, in those who habitually exert it, must be regarded by us doctors as the most adequate and normal of all pacifiers of the mind and calmners of the nerves."[3]

6. RELIGION AND MORALITY

Religious duties are moral obligations dictated by the natural order. Hence an ethical system which eliminates religious duties presents a mutilated morality and omits one of the most important chapters. It is impossible to call one morally good who fails in his duties toward God. If we take religion in this sense we can say morality commands religion.

We may, however, take religion in a wider sense, as embracing all relations of man to God, and then we can say that religion commands morality; for the fulfillment of the moral law is a duty toward God, hence a religious duty, because it is plain that we do not honor God if we flout His law. A moral life is inseparable from sincere religion. Morality is the test of religious sincerity.

In the developing of altruistic sentiment religion has been

[2] *Outlines of a Philosophy of Religion*, p. 27.
[3] *Memories and Studies*, p. 261.

particularly effective. Works of charity do not thrive on the barren soil of irreligion. It would be difficult to mention any great welfare activity inspired by irreligion. As a matter of fact, such purely secular movements as humanitarianism or social service have singularly failed to thrive or attract any great following, not because their ideals were low, but because they lack the life-giving influence of religious inspiration.

Students of the social life are more and more beginning to see the value of religion. Many of them nowadays readily admit and teach that man will never be capable of developing fully his social potentialities without the aid of religion. They are now recognizing the fact that religion releases to their full extent the social instincts, invigorates the consciousness of social responsibility, intensifies the sense of social justice and engenders the spirit of disinterested sacrifice and service without which social cooperation is impossible. Instead of narrowing, religion enlarges man's interests and in this manner proves a powerful instrument of social adaptation. It is the bond that most effectually binds men together. Religion which draws man near to God also draws man nearer to man. It is needless to say, then, that a social order devoid of religion would be utterly lacking in unselfish idealism and social vision. Without religion, the social order would be invaded by individual self-interest and become a barren field dominated by expediency in which neither good will, nor united effort would long endure. It is especially Christianity which has stressed social good will and brought out clearly the social implications of religion. For Christ preaches as His fundamental doctrine the Divine Fatherhood, from which follows as a necessary corollary the brotherhood of man. It is no less than axiomatic to all His teaching that all effort to please God is vain and fraudulent unless it at the same time embraces a like desire to serve the great family of God's children, our fellow men. By the same token no love of man is complete which is not rooted in the deep love of their heavenly Father. Social morality kindled by religion takes on a warmer glow and burns with a brighter passion. It breathes an ardor which no utilitarian or philanthropic motive can impart.

Irreligion often seeks to excuse itself on the plea that a good life is the best service of God. If this is to mean that religion without righteous living is vain, we fully agree. But if it is to mean that it can ever be legitimate to deny God the honor which is due to him, it is contrary to reason. It may be also remarked that the morality of the irreligious rarely rises to a high level and hardly ever gets beyond the plane of external respectability.

7. THE ABUSES OF RELIGION

Though the inward veneration and the love of God can never run to excess, the outward expression of religion can be overdone. Religion can be unduly externalized and divorced from moral living. In that case it turns into hypocrisy and Pharisaism, which bring discredit and ill repute on religion. The cult of false gods as also improper forms of worshiping the true God constitute an abuse of religion. Superstitious practices which consist in seeking to accomplish spiritual ends by purely mechanical means (magic, charms, omens, the prayer mill) are contrary to the right order. Superstition becomes rife when genuine religion decays. Thus Voltaire remarks: "When men get rid of God, they invent some absurdity to take His place." Superstition comes in the wake of irreligion. At this we need not be surprised for the following reason: Irreligion is an utterly irrational attitude; the irreligious man is out of tune with the deepest reality and lacks the most important basic adjustment; in his life everything is out of focus; it is natural that such complete disorientation would bring after it maladjustments in other respects, for unreason breeds unreason and irreligion terminates in superstition. It is not accidental that our age has witnessed a recrudescence of astrology, spiritism, and occult practices, pathetic substitutes for true religion.

Religious ignorance is the source of superstition. Accordingly, the only safeguard against this abuse which dishonors God, degrades man and exposes religion to ridicule, is sound knowledge and an enlightened faith.

8. RELIGIOUS OPTIMISM

Religious optimism has its roots in hope. It is the conviction that moral striving will not be frustrated and that all moral effort will bear fruit. It gives confidence in the battle of life and assures us that, in spite of contrary appearances, God is on the side of right. In virtue of religious hope we know that the good seed sown in the furrows of time will yield an eternal harvest. This hope is necessary to sustain man in his moral struggles and to brace him against the shocks to which he is exposed by the spectacle of the temporary success of the wicked. Uncertainty paralyzes and no one can put his heart into a cause unless he is convinced of its value and future, and the worth-whileness of his own efforts. Nothing so much dispirits man as the prospect of ultimate futility. Unsupported by the moral optimism born of religion man would feel in the presence of an antagonistic universe like a ridiculous pigmy trying to stem the encroaching tide of the sea. On account of its absurdity such a pose could impress no one as heroic. Huxley's concept of morality as a spectacular gladiatorial battle against a hostile order — a defiant war against "the unfathomable injustice of the nature of things" — cannot serve as a challenge but involves a policy of despair. Religious optimism looks at the situation in a truer light; it sees in moral striving a contest in which the omnipotent God himself is our ally and which, therefore, does not go down to defeat.

Pessimism is an implicit denial of the rational government of the world and the justice and goodness of God. It is utterly subversive of morality since it declares the distinction between good and bad without validity, life without meaning and worth, and moral effort futile. Though a few, and

among them Schopenhauer, profess an intellectual pessimism, an emotional pessimism may occasionally creep into
the heart of every man. Against this we must fortify ourselves
by cultivating hope and trust in God.

III

Self-Regarding Duties

1. WHAT MAN OWES TO HIMSELF

Man owes to himself and his Maker that self-fulfillment which is the prerequisite of the attainment of his ultimate end. He must aim at actualizing in himself what constitutes the typical perfection of a human personality. He is under the law of growth and must strive to reach his full moral and spiritual stature. It is his duty to realize the characteristic perfection of his own being. This is the task which he is bound to accomplish out of respect for his own personal dignity and in obedience to his Maker who wants the potentialities with which he has endowed human nature to come to fruition. Thus the duties pertaining to proper self-development are personal duties as well as duties toward God. They are not, however, in the first place duties toward society, though true self-development necessarily redounds to the benefit of society. Man's first business is with himself, for he is not the means for anything else; his primary concern is the culture of his own nature, the development of his best and total self. Our personal perfection is good in itself and for its own sake and not merely because it makes us instruments of social service. Man must be temperate because his rational nature demands it and not primarily that he may be economically efficient. The second follows invariably from the first. A man who lives up to the ideal of personal human excellence does nothing that will impair his social usefulness though he gives no direct thought to the latter. The more a man simply strives to be good, the more will he be able to do good.

The dignity of man lies in his reason; hence typical human perfection requires of man that in all circumstances he act in a rational manner and never forget that reason must be his guide. The attainment and maintenance of true human selfhood is man's essential duty to himself.

The attainment of true human selfhood is accessible to all because it is not contingent on external conditions but only on the good will. It is sufficient if we enter on the way that leads to our perfection and turn our striving toward the objects which make for goodness. If, then, our life is prematurely cut short or adverse circumstances thwart success, perfection will be conferred in the next life in the form of reward. The highest moral selfhood is within reach of everyone who sincerely and perseveringly strives in whatever unfavorable external circumstances his life may be cast. It is the striving that counts and no one is barred from the highest moral achievement. "Better indeed," says Thomas à Kempis in the *Imitation of Christ,* "is an ignorant laborer who serveth God, than a proud philosopher who, neglecting himself, contemplateth the course of the heavens. . . . I had rather feel compunction than know its definition." Even the narrowest life offers opportunities for the realization of the most perfect human selfhood.

2. SELF-RESPECT,   SELF-LOVE,   SELF-DISCIPLINE

The personal duties of man may be basically reduced to self-respect, self-love, and self-discipline.

Self-respect demands of man that he assert his spiritual personality and make it the determining influence in his life; it forbids him to lower himself to the level of a mere sense being which is entirely governed by the impulses arising from the needs of animal nature. To live merely for

sensual gratification is unworthy of a rational being. He who
does not reverence human dignity in himself cannot respect
it in others. Milton speaks of the "inward reverence of a man
toward his own person," reverence for the humanity which
he represents. This reverence for self is enhanced by the
consideration that man bears in himself the divine likeness
which he may not obscure but must bring to its fullest expression. This high regard for one's own dignity is thoroughly consistent with humility for it bears on the ideal and
potential manhood of which we so often fall ignominiously
short. Out of it grow dissatisfaction with our actual achievement, shame, remorse, and self-condemnation.

Self-respect prompts proper care for one's honor and good
name. A good reputation is a great help to righteous conduct
and the fear of disgrace very often lends strong moral support in temptation. Our main concern, however, must be to
be worthy of honor by irreproachable conduct, not to seek
external recognition which we really do not deserve. The
good reputation which we enjoy as a consequence and as the
outward manifestation of our moral integrity also serves as
an encouragement and inspiration to others.

Whilst love of self is a necessary and spontaneous tendency of every being possessed of feeling and consciousness,
well-ordered and properly regulated self-love belongs to the
moral realm. Love of self, when not rightly regulated, rather
tends away from man's true end and genuine good, and
hence according to St. Thomas is the cause of all sin.[1] It is
our duty to love ourselves, not any way, but in the right
manner, that is, to seek our true and genuine good. False
self-love seeks the apparent good which conflicts with our
real well-being. It is obvious that in order to practice dis-
cerning self-love, we must have a right notion of the nature
of the self, which will furnish us the rule and criterion by
which we evaluate the various goods presented to our choice.
Nothing can be more fatal than a false, inadequate, or frag-

[1] *Summa Theol.,* 1, 2, q. 77, a. 4.

mentary conception of the nature and the destiny of the self, since it will blind us to the appreciation of our true good and inevitably result in disastrous choices based on faulty value judgments. We cannot distinguish between our real and fancied interests unless we understand ourselves, know our true needs, and have the right idea of our place in the scheme of the universal order.

Unregulated self-love is selfishness and stands for the partial self against the total self. Its orientation is sensual and material. It is governed by blind impulse and passion, and sees no farther than the interests of the moment. It is harmful to the individual and to society. It may bring fleeting pleasure but can never give deep soul-satisfying happiness. This is well stated by Professor Dewey: "Pleasure is transitory and relative, enduring only while some special activity endures, and having reference only to that activity. Happiness is permanent and universal. It results only when the act is such a one as will satisfy all the interests of the self concerned, or will lead to no conflict, either present or remote. Happiness is the feeling of the whole self, as opposed to the feeling of some one aspect of self."[2]

On the contrary, well-ordered self-love is neither tainted with selfishness nor sensuality, since it is in fundamental harmony with the right order and also has due regard for the objective hierarchy of values. It neither seeks the lower at the cost of the higher nor sacrifices the interests of others to those of the self. It fits the ego into that great moral scheme which is established for the universal good and the welfare of all. Human personality in all is the same, hence he who is true to the law of his own personality is true to the personality of others. The true good of one is never the evil of another. No one can ever promote his own good by conduct that is injurious to others and to society; in a material way, it may benefit him but, in a higher sense, it causes him serious harm. The man who underpays his employees causes

[2] *Psychology,* p. 293.

them misery and suffering but the evil he does to himself is incomparably greater because he stifles something fine within him and his spiritual self shrivels. Moral growth and genuine happiness are never at the expense of others but come about by service and generous sharing. Every time I hinder the self-realization of another I stunt my own personality because man lives not in isolation and only unto himself; his self is intimately interwoven with other selves. Thus whatever violates another self can never be the object of well-ordered self-love. It follows, therefore, that he who stands in the right relation to himself and to God stands in the right relation to his fellow selves. In fact, no one can make a higher contribution to society than a personality whose self-love is regulated and harmonized by the moral law, because a self striving for its true good (the accent, of course, on true) enriches the common life and raises the general moral and cultural level of society, since the real good is never confined to the individual but can always be shared by others. It is like a light which diffuses its radiance. True self-love transcends the individual and embraces also the good of others, the interests of which we feel to be not only identical with, but intimately linked to, our own.

Selfishness, on the other hand, narrows the concept of the good and maims human nature. It puts the self in opposition to other selves and dissociates its interests from theirs but, by becoming the enemy of others, the selfish man becomes his own greatest enemy. A life which selfishly feeds on others is parasitical, and parasitical life is a lower form of life and the very organs which it saves by its fraudulent way of living become crippled and atrophied. Selfishness is disease and deterioration; true self-love is health and growth because it faithfully observes the balance and order which nature prescribes.

The sense nature of man has not immanent within itself a principle of right measure, harmony, proportion, and order; it may war and rebel against the rule of reason. Hence it must be subjected to the law of the spirit which represents the good of the total self; it must be restrained, mastered and, in many cases, its clamorous demands must be denied for only thus can the reign of reason be secured. So self-discipline becomes necessary for man if he is to achieve ideal human selfhood.

Self-control may not be the chief among the virtues but it stands out as the indispensable condition of the true human life, which is such only when it is not determined by blind impulses and momentary feelings but governed by moral purposes and ideals. This condition which constitutes man's worth and is the prerequisite of personal freedom is attained only by the subjugation of the baser inclinations. The rule of reason and will cannot be established if the sensual instincts have not been brought under control. Every virtue presupposes self-control because no virtue exists which does not represent a victory over some contrary tendency of the impulsive, sentient self. Sensual nature must obey, not govern, but in view of its rebellious character subjection to the laws of reason cannot be effected without many struggles.

3. THE SUPREME DUTY OF SELF-LOVE

The master duty to oneself which transcends and comprises all others is to make sure of the one good that alone has absolute and permanent value, eternal salvation. To imperil one's eternal happiness and to expose oneself to everlasting misery is the most flagrant crime against rational self-love. The Lord says: "But one thing is necessary" (Luke 10:42). Sin definitely puts the attainment of our highest destiny in jeopardy; hence the Psalmist exclaims: "He that loveth iniquity hateth his own soul" (Ps. 10:6).

Now the means for the gaining of this end is the constant striving after moral perfection, which involves the proper development of all phases of our being to the full extent of our opportunities.

4. DUTIES REGARDING MENTAL DEVELOPMENT

Reason and will being the directive faculties of man, he is bound to train them in such a way that they will serve him well in the important business of right living. Such appropriate training is effected by education and self-education. In his younger days man must avail himself of the educational opportunities afforded him by the home and the school. To neglect these opportunities may prove a handicap for life and constitute a moral offense. The task of self-education is never completed as long as we breathe, because on earth man never reaches the limit of his mental capacity. Intellectual culture is required by man's dignity and by the intention of the Creator who certainly has not equipped us with unlimited perfectibility to no purpose. Besides, improvement of the mind and the pursuit of knowledge open up unfailing sources of refined enjoyment and produce a distaste for the coarser pleasures of the sense. Mental development, however, must be harmonious and symmetrical and never be dissociated from the supreme purpose of life. Vain curiosity and superficiality are to be avoided for nothing is more dangerous than a mere smattering of knowledge. The half educated are likely to become opinionated, to rely unduly on their own judgment, and to arrive at distorted views of reality.

Basic for intellectual culture is a true knowledge of God, a right interpretation of the meaning of life and a proper understanding of our duties. To eliminate God from knowledge is tantamount to the falsification of truth. He who ignores God can know nothing in its right relation, for God is central in the system of knowledge and essential to the right evaluation of everything else.[3] For the purpose of moral living it is essential to know God as the end of man and the supreme Ruler of the universe, to understand ourselves as

---

[3] Cf. Cardinal Newman, *The Idea of a University.*

spiritual and moral beings with an eternal destiny and to be sufficiently acquainted with the moral law so that we may intelligently plan and direct our lives. This knowledge can be readily acquired by every normal man who seriously reflects on life and takes the pains to make the necessary inquiries.

Intellectual development without a corresponding training of the will is not only useless but harmful. Will culture, accordingly, is likewise a strict obligation of man. Man must acquire such moral habits which will reinforce the will, strengthen it against the allurements of sensuality and enable him to live according to this better knowledge.

The affective side of human nature should not be ignored. Culture of the heart makes for pleasant social relations, contributes to mental peace and aids in the acquisition of social virtues. Graciousness of conduct is inseparable from culture of the heart. Unsubdued passions upset a man's best intentions and rob him of personal charm. Undisciplined feelings and emotions shipwreck many a life and form an occasion of many disagreeable annoyances and exasperating collisions.

5. CARE OF THE BODY

The body is most truly a part of human nature though not most representative and constitutive of the higher self. It is instrumental and subservient to the rational and spiritual life. Physical life is not to be fostered for its own sake; the care bestowed on the body must aim at making it a willing and responsive instrument for the purposes of the rational personality. On account of the imperious and insistent demands of the physical self and the keen pleasure connected with their satisfaction, the interests of the body are likely to be overstressed. On the whole, a severe, even ascetical, attitude toward the body is to be desired. The naturalistic glorification of the body, so common in our day, is contrary to reason and based on a misconception of human nature. The dignity of the body arises from the service it can render in

the attainment of spiritual ends. Mere physical perfection
cannot be the end of a rational being because it would invert
the true order, making reason the servant where it should be
the master. In the human self, the function of the body is
ministerial.

Physical life always has value as the condition of moral
growth and therefore may not be cast aside by suicide. In
the same manner self-mutilation is unlawful because all our
organs offer opportunities for spiritual development and
service. Since, however, physical life is not an end in itself
it may, under proper conditions and restrictions, lawfully
be sacrificed or shortened in the pursuit of a higher aim. A
fireman may find death in the discharge of his duties, and a
scientist may become the victim of research pursued for the
benefit of mankind. The martyr to science is held in great
esteem.

Reasonable care for health is a duty since both our progress in virtue and our social usefulness depend in no small
degree on the preservation of health. Such care implies
moderation in the use of food and drink, appropriate exercise, and sensibly regulated indulgence in innocent forms of
recreation. If we have fallen into sickness it is our duty to
seek restoration of health. In order to effect recovery, it becomes incumbent on us to employ natural remedies or to
engage the services of a competent physician. We are not,
however, required to use extraordinary means for the re-
gaining of health. Extraordinary means are those which involve excessive cost or are associated with unusual pain and
other repugnant features. The use of anesthetics to alle-
viate pain is licit if it does not deprive the patient of the
opportunity of making his peace with heaven and settling
his worldly affairs.

The vices, in addition to their moral deordination, likely
to impair bodily vigor, are gluttony, intemperance, and
unchastity.

The insidiousness of the so-called euphorica consists in

the fact that they produce a more or less pathological mental state characterized by unfounded feelings of well-being, optimism, and efficiency whereas in reality they lower the level of performance. Drugs as mere stimulants are to be condemned without reservation. In regard to alcohol, total abstinence is to be counseled. From the moral point of view the use of alcohol can prove dangerous on the following grounds: moderate use may develop into excessive use; too free an indulgence in alcoholic beverages removes wholesome inhibitions and breaks down habitual moral restraints; lack of moderation, in particular, lowers the tone of social gatherings and tends to produce a relaxing of moral standards. Even tobacco is not without deleterious effects and the safest policy is to shun its use. A sensible person will refuse either to drink or smoke on what is called a dare. Good sportsmanship does not consist in conforming to every suggestion of a crowd and going against one's own better judgment.

6. WORK

By work we understand any significant activity aiming at a useful result. Work may be either mental or manual. From work of some kind no man may rightly dispense himself. He who shirks work leads a parasitical existence. Work is an indispensable factor in self-development and without it physical, mental, and moral deterioration sets in. No man who retains even a shred of self-respect will be satisfied to live on the fruits of the labor of others. The ennobling influences emanating from the industrious pursuit of a useful occupation are incalculable.

Both mental and manual labor are necessary for the good of society. "If," says Bishop P. W. von Keppler in *More Joy,* "there were nobody to perform the menial tasks, the higher culture could not exist." Every kind of work, therefore, should be duly honored. It argues a materialistic concept of life to despise mental labor as unproductive and parasitical,

but contempt for manual labor is equally unreasonable. All
work can be spiritualized and made the medium of personal
self-expression. The manual worker, who is in close contact
with reality, often possesses a remarkably clear judgment,
whereas the mental worker, too exclusively devoted to an
abstract world, is not rarely deficient in practical judgment
and gives evidence of an unharmonious personal development. It is deplorable that in our materialized civilization
many forms of manual labor have become overspecialized
and overmechanized so that they fail to give expression to
man's creative instincts and as a consequence are unable to
give deep satisfaction and the joy that goes with worth-while
performance. Labor should never become degrading but
always offer opportunities for the exercise of mind and body
and the acquisition of true skill.

7.   THE   RIGHT   ATTITUDE   TOWARD
MATERIAL   GOODS

In a general way it may be said that, since man is dependent on external goods, it is his duty to acquire the material
means which are necessary to support himself and his dependents. Shiftlessness and improvidence are particularly
unbecoming a rational being and utterly destructive of character. They have a most demoralizing and degrading effect.
Striving for wealth, however, is in no sense an obligation
since it neither benefits the individual nor society. Our present social evils are chiefly due to an exaggerated seeking of
riches. The proper attitude toward external goods is one
of detachment and indifference because they are only means
and ought to be sought only to the extent that they serve
higher ends. Nothing enslaves men more than a desire for
riches. He who aims at the accumulation of wealth will miss
the finer things of life. The pursuit of riches on account of
its absorbing character will prove a real obstacle to higher
cultural and moral achievement. Those who have greatly
promoted human welfare and contributed to the progress of

civilization have mostly manifested a fine scorn for riches. Inherited wealth has often become a curse to the inheritor and proved his undoing by exempting him from the necessity of earning a livelihood by honest work.

Since the instinct of acquisitiveness is strong in the average individual, our chief duty is to regulate it and keep it within reasonable bounds. The inherent tendency in man is to overestimate earthly possessions and to devote himself too zealously to their acquisition. It is usually a sign of nobility of mind to make little of material goods. Still, it should be borne in mind that the possession of wealth is not necessarily a crime nor poverty in itself a virtue. The happiest condition is that of the man who is compelled to earn his living by useful work which procures for him a frugal, secure, and comfortable existence. He is at once free from the harassing solicitude for his daily bread and the distractions associated with riches. Voluntary poverty deserves our highest respect for those who embrace it do so in order to devote themselves more freely to the service of their fellow men, from whom they expect in return little more than is required to satisfy the bare necessities of life. Particularly today is there a special need to readjust our attitude toward poverty and to recognize it as an invaluable moral aid. For we are a people almost pathological in our dread of being poor. The man who refuses to engage in the mad scramble for riches is out of tune with the mentality of the age and accounted a fool or despised as lacking in the spirit of enterprise, whereas detachment from earthly goods really is an indication of a manly character and an essential condition of true independence.

8. VOCATION

Man must work not only in order to attain to his own personal development but also because he is a member of human society, from which he receives many benefits for which adequate return must be made. Thus work has social implications and becomes service. To gain proficiency it is necessary to devote oneself with permanence to a given line of occupational activity. Hence, there have arisen various states or vocations. In these man finds both opportunities of self-perfection and social service. Thus it is his duty to choose a vocation if his life is not to be trifled away in useless pursuits.

For many the choice of a vocation is very much circumscribed by social conditions. Since, however, in every state we can work out our salvation, we should cheerfully accept such a situation and fill out to the very best of our ability the place that has been assigned to us. Talent and energy find a suitable field of activity in every station of life and when properly applied yield personal satisfaction and social benefit. Fidelity to duty within the sphere of life in which we have been placed is the measure of man's real worth and outranks external success. Beautifully Lessing says: "It is all the same how an honest man makes his living, whether he splits wood or pilots the ship of State; what really matters, in his inmost conscience, is not the thought how useful he is, but to what extent he is willing to make himself useful." In all his labors man can enjoy this elevating sense of useful purpose.

Those who enjoy wider opportunities of choice should not allow themselves merely to drift into a vocation but deliberately choose their work on rational grounds. Guiding considerations should not be ease, comfort, monetary compensation, and social prestige, but regard for our eternal welfare, fitness for the tasks to be undertaken, and social usefulness. Temporal advantages must take a subordinate place. The white-collar job neither offers the greater opportunities for creative self-expression nor affords the fuller satisfaction. Contempt for the artisan, the skilled mechanic, and the craftsman springs from social snobbishness and is no indication of mental superiority. A good trade usually gives greater social security, more independence, intenser joy of living, and richer self-fulfillment than are vouchsafed to the white-collar employee. Overalls should be regarded as a badge of honor and no proficient worker has a reason to be ashamed of his calling. No calling has a monopoly of work that is pleasant and in every one there is drudgery, monotony, and dullness.

The choice of a vocation is a moral question. Man should seek to play a worthy part in life, to make the most of his abilities and to use them in the particular calling in which their exercise will be socially most valuable. There is no merit in the life of the social climber as such. Of course, one should choose an occupation which is congenial. The important thing is that we should be able to feel that the work we are doing and the life we are living are of real value and significance in the world.

9. THE PROFESSION AS SERVICE OF GOD AND OF HUMANITY

Though present in all occupations, the element of service is more conspicuous in the professions. A profession has for its prime object the service it can render to humanity; reward or financial gain should be subordinate consideration. The professional man should be inspired by a high degree of moral idealism and keep free from the taint of commercialism. The privileges which he enjoys have as their counterpart exacting duties. To engage in the practice of a profession without conscientious preparation constitutes a serious moral offense on account of the grave injury that may result from professional ignorance. The humanitarian view does not do full justice to the concept of the profession which, to realize the highest ideal, must be referred to God. Thus Dom Thomas V. Moore writes: "Life is inadequately conceived of as a service to one's fellow men, but such service is rendered more stable and seen in its true light when it is referred ultimately to God and understood as an item of

cooperation by which one does his part in the divine plan
of the universe."[4]

A man's vocation is not merely what he has chosen, it is
also that to which he has been called. It is this lofty thought
which begets generous devotion and full loyalty. The very
word vocation — calling — is expressive of something high,
serious, and solemn. To it there is attached a meaning which
dignifies our work and elevates the labor it entails. It connotes a kind of election to a special kind of task. It intimates that our work, no matter how fortuitously we may
seem to have chosen it, is, in a very true sense, a divine
commission to which God has individually appointed us.
This is the inspiring thought which lends the most menial
toil a dignity and raises it high above the contempt of men.
It is this reverence toward our work which dispels all dis-
sipating thought or contrary ambitions which make us en-
vious of the more remunerative and socially more distinguished positions of others and grow discontented with what
is ours. It is the comforting thought that we are accomplish-
ing God's will which strengthens us to do well the work He
has ordained for us, in spite of our fears that what we do is
of no service or benefaction to ourselves or others. When we
realize that the tasks we fulfill fit into a divine plan, we
cannot but feel that they are invested with real importance
for ourselves and others. If seen in this light all toil becomes glorious and a school of virtue.

10. THE CHOICE OF A VOCATION

Essential factors in the choice of a career are self-knowledge and, more particularly, recognition and acceptance of
one's natural limitations. False ambition is the cause of
choices that lead to self-frustration, to failure, and unhappiness. For ambition when unbridled, causes maladjustment
to one's immediate work and fosters indifference to a present
task by conjuring up dreams of others impossible to one's

[4] Moore, Dom. T. V., *Principles of Ethics*, J. B. Lippincott Co., N. Y., p. 11.

talents and opportunities. Many a man, to put it bluntly, suffers hallucinations about his real role in life and spoils sometimes the good craftsman in him by harboring the vain illusion that his destiny lies in higher spheres. We are too prone to overestimate ourselves and very much inclined to play to the galleries. Instead of self-knowledge and self-acceptance we cultivate self-flattery and self-glorification. Vanity warps our judgment and refuses to accept ourselves as we are because such recognition would prick the inflated notion we have of ourselves and explode the bubble of self-conceit. He who tries to transcend himself courts disappointment. An individual is most contented and most efficient when his task requires the exercise of all his capabilities, and yet is within the range of his accomplishment. A lesser task does not hold his interest or encourage his development, a greater one leads only to discouragement, regret, and not rarely to a physical breakdown induced by worry over the lack of success. Failure, as Lord Bacon tells us, must be attributed not to the love of excellence but to the desire of excelling. Skill in whatever field it may be is something of which a man may rightly feel proud.

11. HISTRIONIC NATURES

There are individuals who live their lives chiefly for a human audience and for the sake of effect. Aptly Goethe has called them "histrionic natures who seem to imagine that they are always in an amphitheatre, with the assembled world as spectators, whereas, all the while they are playing to empty benches." Such a histrionic life, concerned rather with play acting than with honest living, is the very antithesis of the good life and is likely to turn into downright hypocrisy. The applause of the multitude is no guarantee of moral worth for its judgments are very fallacious and more calculated to draw us down than to prove a spur to nobler endeavor. The memory, however, of the all-seeing Eye that is ever upon us and of the invisible choir of the saints will make us try to be, and not merely to play a role. Hence, if we staged our life consciously before an audience of the world's great ones and submitted our performance to the scrutiny of their uncompromising judgment, we might derive immense benefit and greater inspiration to play our part more carefully in order to win their wholehearted approval. In this sense St. Paul says: "We are made a spectacle to the world and to the angels and to men" (I Cor. 4:9). In moral life there can be no masquerading. Unearned honors confer no moral worth. Truly G. Flaubert says: "There are undeserved honors which dishonor."

It is well known that wealth often becomes a subtly corrupting influence. The same can be said of honors, dignities, and high social position, especially if they have been eagerly sought. An ancient saw declares: "Honors change morals." And the change is rarely for the better.

Unimpressed, as the sincerely striving man should be, by the acclaim of the crowd, he should not be insensible to the criticism of his fellow men. Ordinarily we profit more by criticism than by praise. The man who never hears the voice of criticism is truly unfortunate for he acquires a false outlook on life and dwells in a phantastic world of his own creation. It is the misfortune of the great to become wrapped in clouds of incense created by the flattery and adulation of those who are looking for favors.

IV

Duties of Man to Man

---

1. WHAT WE OWE ONE ANOTHER

We have at some length dwelt on the self-regarding duties because the duties to our fellow men are patterned after the former. The reason for this is to be sought in the essential equality of men. My fellow man like myself possesses the same human nature which in him I must respect as in myself; he is a personal self, entitled to the same inviolability which I claim for myself; he is endowed with the same rights and the same dignity and shares the same destiny; he moreover feels a wrong as keenly as I do. On this essential equality the negative duties toward our fellow men are based, expressed in the rule: Do to no man what you would not have men do to you.

But men are not isolated, dwelling apart and shut off one from another. They are linked together in a network of intimate relations; they constitute a community of selves, living under the law of reciprocity and mutual dependence; they need one another and therefore are bound to mutual helpfulness. This positive aspect of our duties to others is embodied in the other rule which says: "Whatsoever you would that men should do to you, do you also to them" (Matt. 8:12). Hence, it is not enough to refrain from injuring others; we are also held actually to promote their welfare in the same manner, though not in the same degree, as we seek our own good.

It is the special merit of Christianity to have made the law of neighborly love central in morality. It has made humanity a brotherhood and the world a neighborhood. It has universalized the concept of neighbor which before its advent was restricted to the members of the tribe or the nation. It has broken down the barriers between men and proclaimed them one great family of brothers. It teaches us to include our fellow men in our prayers. It has sanctified service. "Christianity," writes Dr. Seth, "has done much to bring home to the human mind the essential dignity and high privilege of service, and to teach us how, in serving our fellows and in bearing one another's burdens, we may find the path of perfect self-realization."[1] It has shattered the pagan ideal of pride, megalomania, self-sufficiency, arrogance, and pompous self-complacency.

The individual must transcend himself. Life is meant to be a fellowship, a sharing, a vital comradeship, a living and working together. In that direction lies the true self-fulfillment. Such a life liberates from the narrow prison house of selfishness. The self-centered individual is imprisoned within himself, is incredibly miserable and stunted in all the finer qualities of manhood. Love is life; selfishness is death. "He that loveth not, abideth in death" (I John 3:14).

Love of neighbor is not an emotional mood luxuriating in itself, not a flabby sentiment, but a dynamic will to help, expressing itself in deeds. It is not a mere feeling of vague good will directed toward everybody in general but never turning in actual helpfulness to anybody in particular. Sentimentality may move to tears but will issues in actions and seeks concrete ways of relieving suffering. Sympathy is good only when it becomes active.

2. THE DUTY OF CHARITY

Charity implies benevolence and beneficence. As self-love so also love of neighbor must be well ordered so that we

[1] *A Study of Ethical Principles*, p. 264.

place his spiritual and eternal good first. Sins against the spiritual good of our neighbor are seduction, scandal, and cooperation in his evil deeds. We can further the spiritual welfare of others by good example, counsel, instruction, and encouragement. To succor a fellow man in extreme spiritual necessity, that is, to save him from the imminent danger of losing his soul we are bound to make heroic efforts and even to risk our life. To relieve his corporal needs we must be ready to incur sacrifices proportionate to the seriousness of the necessity.

3. THE ORDER OF CHARITY

Neighborliness has degrees. To some we are bound by closer ties than to others; it is reasonable that the claims of the former should have precedence over those of the latter. To override the priority of those standing to us in nearer relationships does not make for the general good. The superior title of blood relationship must not arbitrarily be set aside. Any man who wantonly violates this prior claim of his own kin upon his charity and gives to a stranger what he denies his own needy relations upsets the proper order and acts contrary to the dictates of the natural law. For every man by the natural tie that binds him in blood to his father and mother, family and relatives as well as those of his own household is bound to assist them in preference to others who have no such claim upon him. Such a doctrine is patently consonant with the most fundamental instincts of human nature.

4. VARIOUS OFFENSES AGAINST CHARITY

Ugly offenses against the love which we owe our fellow men are defamation of character, detraction, slander, revelation of their hidden faults, or anything which injures their reputation. It is a strict duty of justice to restore the good name that has been injured. False testimony is a particularly odious crime. Great harm can be done by uncharitable gossip. To avoid outer offenses in this line it is essential to guard against internal violations of charity such as envy, suspicion, and rash judgment, for these are the evil seeds from which uncharitable words and acts grow. Secret crimes may be revealed if the good of another or the common welfare demand it.

We have no right to pry into the secrets of another or to bare them. To expose the secrets of another may be an extremely cruel act and cause much unhappiness. Even the law regards certain communications as enjoying a privileged character and recognizes the professional secret. Public authority, however, can dispense from the obligation of secrecy by order of a court of justice. There is only one secret which binds absolutely and under all circumstances, the sacramental seal of the confessional. Letters should be regarded as sacrosanct. Parents may read the letters of children still under their authority.

5. MENTAL CRUELTY

Many men of coarser grain are insensitive to the pain which they constantly inflict on their environment by their arrogance, lack of consideration, incessant driving, and exacting demands. They show no appreciation, bestow no praise, are given to faultfinding, and can see only their way of doing things. They begrudge others the harmless pleasures which they do not care to enjoy themselves. Such an attitude becomes the source of perpetual annoyance and misery to others. The closer the contacts the more intense is the suffering. Mental cruelty, resulting from an undisciplined and selfish nature and a domineering temperament, wrecks the happiness of many a home and causes many a marriage to end in failure. It embitters the lives of our neighbors and produces refined tortures. There is no excuse for it.

Moral idealism makes some indifferent to the real exigencies of life and to live in an abstract world. Nothing can justify indifference to the comfort and feelings of those with whom we live. In fact, we must admit that it is the grave error of many well-meaning idealists that they become so absorbed in their favorite theory that they are blind to reality and its just claims. An idealism which ruthlessly sacrifices the actual is a perverted idealism. Carlyle is but a distinguished example of one who lived to condemn himself severely for his brusque indifference to the lesser but vital charities of home life. Gruffness and irritability are in the world's eyes glaring moral defects which seriously impugn all other religious excellence. A man should not in the zeal of his idealism permit himself to become disinterested in the ordinary affairs of life. Such excess cannot but breed general disdain for the man and excite contempt for all idealism as a misguided enthusiasm.

6. ALMSGIVING

While charity demands that those who enjoy abundance relieve the distress of the needy, indiscriminate almsgiving is not to be encouraged. Material assistance should be given in such a way that it contributes toward the social rehabilitation of the recipient. For the majority who neither have the time nor the ability to study the merits of a case the best way of discharging their obligations of charity will be to support according to their means accredited welfare agencies of the community. The truly charitable man, however, will not be satisfied with vicarious charity but will seek opportunities to minister personally to the deserving poor. Genuine need must always find us responsive to its prayers. Those on the sunny side of life should always be mindful of the sorry plight of the underprivileged and extend a helping hand to those familiar with want and misfortune. Dr. Paulsen reminds us that refusal to proffer help at a critical juncture in life may thrust an unfortunate fellow man into deeper misery; "How many a criminal may trace the beginning of his career to unkind, repellant treatment in misfortune! If a helping hand had been extended at the right moment, it might have saved a human soul from destruction. It was not offered; the first step on the wrong path was taken and drew all the others after it, until the road ended in the penitentiary."[2]

7. LOYALTY TO THE TRUTH

In one sense truthfulness is a self-regarding duty inasmuch as we must strive to cultivate intellectual honesty, open-mindedness, sincerity, and a desire to advance in knowledge. We must not allow personal interest and likes or dislikes to sway our judgment and vitiate our reasoning. Rationalization, that is, the twisting of the truth to suit our wishes, is intellectual dishonesty. Locke somewhere remarks: "There is one unerring mark by which a man may know whether he is a lover of truth in earnest, viz., the not entertaining any proposition with greater assurance than the proofs it is built on will warrant." He who is honest with himself in this way will also be honest in dealing with others, as the advice in Shakespeare's *Hamlet* has it:

> To thine own self be true,
> And it must follow as the night the day,
> Thou canst not then be false to any man.

Truth is a good of a high order and should be the guide of our conduct. Error leads to harmful activity and is the source of the many evils that afflict mankind. All human misery began with a lie. Lying stands out as a great moral wrong. The dissemination of an error constitutes a serious crime against humanity. In the acquisition of truth we are largely dependent on our fellow men and the means by which truth is communicated is speech. Briefly we may state: Speech is the natural instrument of truth and it is perverted if it is deliberately converted into a vehicle of falsehood.

There is an intrinsic deordination in lying. This follows

[2] Paulsen, F., *A System of Ethics*, Charles Scribner's Sons, N. Y., p. 652.

from the following consideration: By its very nature the purpose of speech is to manifest the mind. It is a social device and renders communication between men possible. When a man speaks to us, we take it that it is his intention to reveal his thoughts to us. We expect therefore conformity between the words of the speaker and the content of his mind. Word and thought belong together; the word is the outward sign of the thought. A lie runs counter to this essential and natural relation. Patently, therefore, lying cannot but be regarded as the abuse of a function and the frustration of its obvious purpose. From this basic perversion, the evil social consequences of lying flow with logical necessity; speech is meant to be a social bond; the lie which falsifies the nature of speech becomes socially disruptive. A formal lie is an intended discrepancy between one's utterance and one's thought, or briefer, speaking against one's mind. Manifestly, the intention of deceiving is invariably present in a lie. Of course, lying can be done by writing, gesture, or action as well as by speech. The lie takes on an added malice if it implies an injustice. It reaches its highest malice in perjury, in which the God of Truth is invoked as the witness of falsehood. Perjury has everywhere and always been considered as one of the greatest crimes, as a sign of extreme viciousness and baseness; the Greeks looked upon it as the most heinous crime. Hence, the prevalence of perjury in our days is an alarming symptom of the moral corruption of contemporary society.

8. THE EVILS OF LYING

Lying has disastrous consequences both for the individual and society. Untruthfulness is destructive of moral stamina. It brings many other vices in its train and breaks down resistance to moral delinquency because it holds out the promise of immunity from punishment. The liar foolishly imagines that he can escape the consequences of his wrongdoing. Respect for the truth is the core of manliness; as long as it

persists moral regeneration can be effected. The cultivation
of truthfulness is the first step in the building of moral
strength. The lie is the easy resort of the coward and makes
for spiritual flabbiness. Punishment which is too severe may
lead to the formation of lying habits. He who confesses a
fault should be respected and treated with leniency because
he has already in his heart dissociated himself from his mis-
deed. Unduly stern and unrelenting parents may start their
children on the downward road of habitual untruthfulness.

The social effects of lying are most harmful. If it becomes
prevalent, lying destroys the mutual confidence necessary for
social life. It creates a poisonous atmosphere of distrust
which adversely affects all human relations and produces between man and man a suspicious aloofness. Its corrosive
effect may be likened to that of spurious coinage which
makes men chary in money transactions. The counterfeiter
not only causes loss to the individual who receives the spurious coin but brings into disrepute the genuine currency of
the realm which ought to pass from hand to hand with implicit trust and without hesitation. Thus lying discredits the
intellectual medium of exchange and makes man distrustful
of the words of his fellows. Falsehood is particularly destructive when it enters the intimate spheres of the home, friendship and the school, in which spontaneous trust should
prevail.

Low forms of lying are flattery, adulation, and sycophancy;
they corrupt the great, the rich, and the powerful and betray
the interests of those who are the victims of arrogance, arbitrariness, and misrule. The insolence of those in power
grows by the base flattery of the unscrupulous who profit by
their fawning servility.

9. POSITIVE SIDE OF VERACITY

Though lying is morally objectionable, outspokenness and
plain speech are not necessarily virtuous. The telling of the
truth must be prompted by charity and accompanied by

tact. Unthinking bluntness of speech without regard to the effect on the thoughts and feelings of others deserves no praise and may manifest nothing more than an utter absence of wisdom, justice, kindness, and temperance. So-called candor very often veils malice and a desire to hurt. Reserve in speech and reticence are admirable character traits. What goes for frank criticism may be only the outcome of mental cruelty which takes delight in the discomfiture of another and in belittling achievements which are not his own.

Those who are professionally engaged in the public communication of the truth are in a special manner bound by the law of veracity. To this category belong teachers, lecturers, writers, scientists, historians, and newspapermen. They should regard their calling as a service of the truth and realize their responsibility to the public which depends on them for right information. Nothing could be more damnable than to convert the service of the truth into a conspiracy against the truth. Only reliable information and scrupulously verified knowledge should be transmitted. To distort the truth in the interests of propaganda is a dastardly crime against society.

Truth, however, is not always beneficial. The minds of men are not always prepared for the truth and in that state knowledge would not serve them well. In the dissemination of information pedagogical considerations must be taken into account. Truth must be communicated in judicious doses in which it will not work harm. Men lacking judgment will put a false construction on the truth and wrest it to their own undoing. The telling of the whole truth may at times be very inopportune and in the interests of the common welfare the truth may have to be temporarily withheld. Truth sometimes is dynamite and must be carefully handled.

10. MENTAL RESERVATION

Lying, being intrinsically wrong, can never be sanctioned, yet the concealment of the truth may become a moral obligation. There must be a morally unobjectionable way to meet this delicate situation. The expedient of silence may not be serviceable as silence would too readily be construed as consent. A refusal to answer the question would confirm suspicion. An answer must be given which will protect the secret or the dangerous truth and distract the attention of the inquirer by satisfying his curiosity. This can be effected only by positive affirmation or plain denial as the case may be. In the predicament, then, when we are asked concerning a secret which we have no right to divulge or which the inquirer has no right to know, or when information is sought which would result in injury, we may have recourse to a mental reservation, a manner of speech incomplete in itself and to be supplemented and interpreted according to the whole situation. The face value of the statement is modified and limited by a restriction which the speaker does not disclose but which would be manifest to anyone who considers the circumstances in their entirety and their trying character. The mental reservation, therefore, does not so much deceive as make the importunate questioner, who, in his eagerness to find out what he has no legitimate claim to know, overlooks important aspects of the case, deceive himself. The mental reservation cannot be made an ordinary policy but is permissible only when one is unduly pressed by an unauthorized and persistent questioner; it presupposes the right to withhold the information desired.

A purely mental reservation, of which the external circumstances give no indication and which uses words in a totally arbitrary sense, differs in no way from a lie and is morally indefensible.

11. CONTRACTUAL OBLIGATIONS

A contract is a mutual agreement which creates an obligation in justice. To be binding it must bear on what is morally lawful and be entered into with knowledge and freedom. In making contracts misrepresentations must be avoided because they would violate justice and veracity. The duties assumed should be honestly complied with. Positive law regulates practically all contracts and to these regulations the contracting parties must conform.

12. FREEDOM OF ACTION

We may not interfere with the actions of our neighbor unless they infringe on our rights. Such restriction can only come from lawful authority. It would, however, be right to restrain a fellow man from committing a serious crime, such as suicide or assault upon another.

13. INJURY TO PROPERTY

We must respect the material possessions of our fellow men and not disturb them in the enjoyment of the property which they have acquired. If material damage has been inflicted willfully, indemnification becomes obligatory. Theft is an offense both against charity and justice. Its gravity depends on the amount stolen. To take from a poor person an object even of small value may involve mortal guilt. Though no absolute rule can be established, in ordinary conditions a day's wage may be looked upon as constituting grave matter. In a series of thefts the separate items coalesce. To delay the paying of bills, especially where small tradesmen are concerned, may cause great inconvenience and is very reprehensible. It is hard to find words severe enough to brand properly the conduct of those who make servants, laborers, dressmakers, seamstresses, and other hired employees wait, without a very good reason, for their wages. This may very often be mere thoughtlessness but it bears the earmarks of callousness and heartless selfishness. Prompt payment of wages prevents much disappointment and suffering. In Deuteronomy we read: "Pay him the price of his labor the same day" (24:15).

V

Private Ownership

1. BASIS FOR THE RIGHT OF PRIVATE PROPERTY

The institution of private property has its roots in human nature and the exigencies of society. In view of this, Victor Cathrein, S.J., says in his *Moral Philosophy:* "The first reason for the institution of private ownership is the moral impossibility of any other system of ownership." The right of self-determination which goes with a rational personality implies the right to acquire external goods and to use them according to one's own judgment and choice. Only private ownership of the things necessary for the maintenance of life guarantees the freedom and independence required by human dignity. Nothing less than private property will serve as a sufficient incentive to put forth one's best efforts. Not to be permitted to appropriate and dispose of the fruits of one's labor discourages industry and ultimately will diminish the output of national production. It stifles initiative and kills individual enterprise. It takes the joy out of work and leaves no other motive but that of external coercion. Private ownership is also socially beneficial for it is the only arrangement which secures efficient and economical management of productive capital. There is an intimate relation between man and the product of his creative labor; man stamps what his work brings forth with the imprint of his own personality; it should therefore belong to him and be subject to his will to which it owes its being. True human progress and full cultural development are predicated on private ownership. Private ownership increases the consciousness of responsibility so essential for a genuinely social life and the welfare of the community. Order, peace, general well-being, civilization are linked with the institution of private ownership, and communities in which it is abolished will be reduced to impoverishment. History affords no instance of an advanced civilization based on communistic ownership. Even small communities in which common ownership was practiced have had but a precarious existence and after some time have disintegrated. Personality needs as its outward, concrete embodiment private property. Hence, V. Brants correctly remarks: "To give up private ownership, one must be either above or below human normalcy." We sum the argument up in the words of Father Valere Fallon, S.J.: "Private ownership, therefore, arises as the guarantee of liberty, peace, order in society, and as the means of securing an intense, progressive, and economical development of the resources which nature has prepared for us."[1]

The right of ownership is not derived from the State for the State is not the first owner, since the individual is prior to political organization and reserved goods for his personal use before any State had been formed. Because private property is so completely in accord with the requirements of human nature and so well adapted to promote social welfare, and on the other hand its negation fraught with such sinister possibilities, we may confidently assert that it is derived from the natural law. It seems to have a stronger foundation than mere expediency.

The present-day attacks on private ownership are due to its distortion and abuse, which have nullified the right for great numbers of the community. The very fact that the prevailing economic order defrauds so many of this right proclaims its essential immoral tendency and has led to the

---

[1] *Principles of Social Economy,* p. 194.

awful indictment voiced by Proudhon: *La propriété, c'est le vol.*" (Property is theft.) However much we may condemn the unjust distribution of property in our days, we cannot admit that collectivistic ownership would be a considerable improvement. The remedy lies in a wide diffusion of private property which would make the right of ownership effective for all.

2. LIMITATIONS OF PRIVATE PROPERTY

Property rights are essentially limited. Private ownership must not frustrate the original and primary destination of the earth to serve the needs of mankind. In fact, the justification of any concrete form of property holding lies in this that it accomplishes that end better than any other system would do. Accordingly, as a given system fails to minister to the needs of all, it forfeits its title to existence. The first restriction on ownership comes from the rights of others who are entitled to share in the goods of the earth. Unequal fortunes are not only legitimate but desirable; excessive inequalities, however, are contrary to the intentions of nature. A defense of the principle of private ownership can in no sense be construed as an apologia for the concentration of wealth in the hands of a few — the outstanding trait of the actual distribution of property under the existing regime. The inherent restriction on ownership derives from the purpose of property which is to administer to the needs of the owner; now since no man has unlimited needs, he can have no right to an unlimited amount of goods for his own private satisfaction. On all ownership lies a social responsibility which requires that all property be used in a socially beneficial manner. It is the divorce of ownership from its social obligations, which was brought about by economic liberalism, that has resulted in the maldistribution of property now afflicting society.

The theory of private ownership intends to benefit all; it is perverted if it is made to serve only the interests of the few. The ideal condition at which it aims would be that all should enjoy property rights which would enable them to provide adequately for themselves.

It is the office of the State to promote the common good and it is therefore its duty to regulate ownership in a manner consonant with the best interests of all. The advocates of private ownership do not hold that all things must be privately owned; on the contrary, they readily agree that public ownership with regard to certain things is expedient in order to forestall abuses. Thus Pius XI says in the encyclical *Quadragesimo Anno:* "For it is rightly contended that certain forms of property must be reserved to the State, since they carry with them an opportunity of domination too great to be left to private individuals without injury to the community at large." The theory of private ownership asserts that the State must not be the sole owner; it does not deny that it might and should also be an owner.

3. LABOR AS A TITLE TO THE ACQUISI- TION OF PROPERTY

In the course of historical development access to property has become more and more restricted. For all practical purposes the title of occupation has become obsolete because hardly a foot of ground can be found which does not already belong to someone. Thus it would appear that the late-comers are permanently debarred from the possession of property. As a matter of fact, we have with us a numerous propertyless class, which depends for the means of subsistence entirely on the work of their hands and the services they render to those who are more fortunately circumstanced. Still, if private ownership is a right closely bound up with human personality, the opportunity for the acquisition of property other than is required for daily consumption should always remain open to man at whatever period of history he may happen to be born. Consequently labor must be made the means of acquiring real property; the worker must be enabled to become a property holder in his own right. In other words, wages must be such that they make it possible for the worker not only to continue his existence as a worker or wage earner, but to ascend into the class of property owners. The status of the proletarian should not be a permanent one, for it is only when the transition from one class to another meets no unsurpassable barriers that class consciousness and class hatred cannot arise. This view is held both by Leo XIII and Pius XI. We adduce them here not as custodians of revealed truths but as exponents of the dictates of natural justice. The former writes: "If working people can be encouraged to look forward to obtaining a share in the land, the consequence will be that the gulf between vast wealth and sheer poverty will be bridged over, and the respective classes will be brought nearer to one another. The law, therefore, should favor ownership and its policy should be to induce as many as possible of the humbler class to become owners" (*Rerum Novarum*). To which the latter adds: "This program cannot, however, be realized unless the propertyless wage earner be placed in such circumstances that by skill and thrift he can acquire a certain moderate ownership. We deem it advisable that the wage contract should, when possible, be modified somewhat by a contract of partnership, as is already being tried in various ways to the no small gain both of the wage earners and of the employers" (*Quadragesimo Anno*). Not the abolition of private property, which Communism demands, not the restriction of ownership to a few, as it exists under liberalistic Capitalism, but the wide distribution and diffusion of private property is the form of property holding most fitted to human nature and most conducive to social progress and stability.

VI

Social Morality

---

1. SOCIAL DUTIES

Social duties affect men inasmuch as they are members of a society and envisage the common good for the attainment of which the society exists. Social organization gives rise to specifically new relations on which duties are grafted that differ essentially from those pertaining to individual morality. Society is a unit or a whole and is more than a nominal and shadowy reality; still it does not possess substantial being as an organism and the individual is not completely absorbed by it. Man, though a member of society, retains a sphere of activity that belongs to him as a person. It has always been difficult to delimit the sphere of personal activity from that of social activity. There have always existed opposite tendencies, the one asserting an excessive individualism, the other proclaiming an exaggerated socialism. Man is not only a part of a social body, he is also a self in his own right. Society must not blot out the individual and reduce him merely to the status of a part.

The unity of society is a unity of order; it is moral not physical. It is not a thing distinct from the associated individuals; it is they themselves. Wrong conceptions of the nature of society lead to the most deplorable social policies as the present amply testifies. Society is for man and not man for society. The good of society cannot be separated from the good of the individual.

It is well to realize the difficulty from the outset in order
to avoid excesses in either direction and to induce caution.
In determining, therefore, the respective spheres of man's
personal and social life, it is essential to bear in mind that
man is a complex being and that there are two aspects to his
nature, of neither of which we must lose sight. At once man
is autocentric and heterocentric, that is, he lives unto himself and for society. To embrace these two truths in one focal
point of view and to harmonize them calls for a persistent
effort of attention. To set forth the double aspect in the right
manner requires careful choice of terms and a continual
balancing of statement against statement.

At some point the individual transcends society; there is
an intimate personal life which he lives for himself and into
which society cannot enter. Not all his life is the corporate
life of the community. True, society has a corporate activity
but outside of this corporate activity, individuals carry on a
personal activity of their own. No one says this clearer than
St. Thomas: "The unity formed by the whole which is called
the state or the family is a unity of co-ordination, not a
simple unity. Each element of the social whole has its activity which is not that of the whole; the whole itself has also,
as such, an operation proper to it."[1] Not all man's activity is
political, directed toward political ends and regulated by
political authority. There is an activity which society exerts
through the individual and which constitutes a truly social
function; this activity patently must be directed by the social
body and social authority, for it is plain that the ends and
functions of the whole cannot be determined by the parts.
All activities aiming at the common welfare come under the
jurisdiction of the State. In matters which bear on his own
personal good, man remains his own master under God.
Manifestly everything which is connected with the eternal
end of man falls into this category since the State is concerned only with temporal welfare. The State belongs only
to time; man belongs also to eternity.

[1] I. *Eth.* I.

2. NATURE OF SOCIETY

A society is a moral and stable union of a number of persons striving toward a common end in a concerted manner. The bond which holds these individuals together is the common end and the agency which directs their actions in regard to the end is authority. Authority is indispensable in a society. It may be defined as the right of obligating and coercing the various members of society to do or not to do certain things, so that in a harmonious way they may cooperate for the attainment of the end of society. Ethics is interested only in those societies which with necessity grow out of the nature of man and the duties and essential constitution of which are defined by the natural law. These are the domestic society, the civil society, and the international society.

The Church in the supernatural order is a society in its own right deriving its authority from its Divine Founder.

Free societies rest on agreement and are subject to the moral laws which govern contracts. Men have an inherent right to form associations for the attainment of legitimate ends. On this ground we uphold the right of labor to organize for the purpose of securing what is due to the laborer and of bettering the economic and social condition of the worker. It is the duty of the State not only to allow labor unions but also to give them adequate protection in law. The right of free association can be curbed by civil authority only to the extent that it is employed in the pursuit of an immoral purpose, conflicts with the rights of others, or imperils the common good. A flourishing free associational life is socially beneficial, promotes culture, and makes for general contentment.

3. THE STATE

Though the State in the natural order is the only perfect and self-sufficient society, it is not, and cannot be, the only

association and consequently may neither substitute itself
for all other associations nor merge them completely in itself.
This would be the end of culture and sound the death knell
of freedom. We conclude, therefore, that the claims of
Totalitarianism, which propose to absorb the entire life of
the individual and to force the life of the community into an
arbitrary and uniform mold, are contrary to the natural law.
In this connection St. Thomas observes: "Man is not subservient to the civil authority to the extent of his whole
self."[2] Commenting on these words, J. Rickaby, S.J., remarks in *Political and Moral Essays:* "This I take to be a
very pregnant saying. It cannot be denied that the best work
of the artist, of the scientist, of the scholar — not to say the
saint — is done without any conscious reference to civil society and away from civil control." In fact, it is difficult to
conceive the meaning of scholarly research conducted for
the sake of political purposes and carried on under political
supervision. It is amusing to think of what might become of
history, social philosophy, and the study of law, under these
circumstances.

[2] *Sum. Theo.,* 1, 2, 21, 4.

VII

Social Institutions

1. SOCIAL NATURE OF MAN

We can find the true attitude toward social institutions only if we have the right notion of the social nature of man. Unless we understand man to be essentially social, social life will be conceived of as a limitation and a restraint whereas, in reality, it is the condition of personal self-fulfillment. To say that man is by nature social is the same as saying that there are certain personal goods which are obtainable for man only by cooperation in an established social order. The isolated man, if he is thinkable at all, would be barred from that higher human perfection which can be secured only if man becomes a member of a social unit which aims especially at the realization of that aspect of personality for which it exists. We speak of this end as the common good because it is shared by other selves which cooperate in its production. It is a higher good than they could have produced separately but all participate in it. Man is not less a man for being a member of a society but it is only as such a member that he can fully become a man.

Man, then, is by nature social. The primitive asocial or antisocial man of Rousseau and Hobbes is a figment of the imagination. The individual is not sufficient to himself. He needs society for his proper development. A truly human existence is impossible except in society. Man loses nothing in society but gains infinitely. Man's social nature is indicated by the ineradicable instinct for human fellowship, his utter dependence on his fellow men, his sympathetic and altruistic emotions, the gift of speech, the long period of training which he requires, and the universal fact of association. Everything urges man to social living: his needs, his tastes, his inclinations, his advantage. A state of society is his natural habitat for which the Creator has unmistakably destined him.

Society, then, is not an artificial arrangement to be put together in an arbitrary and mechanical manner. It is held together by multiple spiritual bonds and material interests and cannot be broken up into unrelated departments as the individualistic theory would have it. Though not an organism, it possesses an organic structure and between the State and the individual many intermediary formations intervene. The atomistic conception of society which would make of the State merely a collection, a juxtaposition, or a sum of individuals, neither corresponds to the actual facts nor is it borne out by historical development.

If society is an order, it produces inequalities, for in an order, as in a structural unit, not all can be alike. The social inequalities are for the common good and do not imply any personal inferiority. We have seen that the individual transcends society; hence his social status need not affect his personal worth.

2. SOCIAL INSTITUTIONS

Association is more than mere gregariousness, which is also found in those animals which live in herds, for in the latter we have no rational cooperation. Man builds up social institutions to attain to the goods which otherwise would not be within his reach. An institution represents an objective good or value which man appropriates to himself by entering into the institution and accepting the mode of life which it imposes. Marriage offers benefits which cannot be obtained outside of this social state. The various natural social institutions objectively represent human values and man, entering into them, lives on a higher human plane and enjoys a richer personal development.

3. THE FAMILY

Domestic society is the first and most basic society. The essential structure of this society is given by the natural law. Man cannot fashion it to suit himself. Through it certain well-defined ends are to be realized and these ends call for certain means.

Domestic society is based on marriage. Marriage is the stable union of man and woman, involving their living together with a view to the procreation and rearing of offspring. Human propagation can be carried on decently only under the form of monogamous and permanent marriage. Its properties, unity and indissolubility, are determined by nature itself. The intimacy of the marriage relation excludes anything like promiscuity. The interests of the offspring demand indissolubility. These properties are essential for otherwise the ends of matrimony would be defeated. The frustration of the primary end of marriage by birth control, i.e., prevention of conception by artificial means, is condemned by the moral law and constitutes an ugly abuse of marriage.

Human happiness and progress depend on the home. Whatever endangers the home and destroys the integrity of the family life is harmful to human society. That divorce is a menace to our national existence is being more and more recognized. Broken homes to a large extent account for the growing juvenile delinquency which alarms observers of our times. The duties of the parents are to promote order in the home and to care for the physical and spiritual well-being of those entrusted to their care. From these solemn duties emanate certain inviolable parental rights on which public authority may not encroach. Parental authority ceases when the young people have reached an age in which they should assume responsibility for their own lives. As long as they continue to live under the parental roof they are bound to that degree of obedience which is necessary to maintain peace, order, and harmony in the household. It goes without saying that children are never dispensed from the duty of gratitude, love, respect, and practical helpfulness.

On the family depends not only the physical perpetuation of society, but likewise its moral growth. From this focal point social sentiment radiates and diffuses itself in ever widening circles through the nation. The social importance of the domestic society is strongly emphasized by Leo XIII when he writes: "The family is the cradle of civil society, and it is largely within the confines of the domestic hearth that is prepared the destiny of nations." From this, the enormous influence of woman, who is chiefly the homemaker, can readily be gauged.

Since the marriage state involves great responsibilities it should not be entered thoughtlessly and frivolously. Those who contemplate this grave step ought to prepare themselves for the duties which they are about to assume. The most important factor in making married life successful is moral character.

The obligation to marry is not a universal one. Celibacy, therefore, is not contrary to the natural law but if accepted for a high moral purpose is meritorious. There is, however, also a selfish celibacy which has no merit.

VIII

The State

1. CIVIL SOCIETY

Civil society or the State is the ultimate of association in the natural order. It is a complete, self-sufficient, and perfect society. There is a completeness and fullness about the end which it pursues, and it possesses within itself the means necessary for the attainment of its end. It is not the part of another society nor in the pursuit of its own aims subordinated to another society; hence, it is invested with the attribute of sovereignty. Other societies aim at the realization of partial aspects of man's good, the State seeks in a comprehensive and inclusive manner his entire temporal welfare. Within it the other necessary or free human societies of an incomplete nature exist and are protected and fostered. It may be defined as a perfect and self-sufficing society consisting of many families united under a common ruler for the attainment of the complete temporal welfare and life of the community.

The family is sufficient neither to provide adequately for all the needs of man nor to maintain and protect itself. Accordingly families combine to form larger social units in which the more abundant life can be realized. They grow into the civil society, the purpose of which is not to be substituted for the family but rather to assist the family better to fulfill its own function and to accomplish its tasks. The function of the State in regard to the family consequently is essentially a protective one. The State cannot arbitrarily regulate family life because the family exists prior to it and the essential conditions of the conjugal and domestic society are determined by the natural law. The intimate atmosphere of the family is also better adapted to a personal ministry which the larger and impersonal social unit could only imperfectly render. Precisely because the family is a unit smaller than the State it exercises an influence more intense and more profound. In this narrow circle the members are drawn closely together both by intimate personal contact and a community of interests, and in this manner are imbued with a social spirit which later will be extended to wider circles; so it becomes the first socializing influence in the individual's life. Instead of tightening the mutual ties between the members of society, the destruction of the personal intimacy of the home would disrupt them and rob society of its organic character.

The combination of many families is necessary to render possible that division of labor and diversity of function required for culture and civilization.

2. AUTHORITY   IN   THE   STATE

Civil authority has its source in the natural order and ultimately in the will of God. A common life and harmonious cooperation would be impossible without an effective authority. Anarchy would plunge mankind into chaos and confusion and reduce it to a state of savagery. Hence, God, who wants a well-regulated and fruitful social life, also wants political authority. This theory which derives political power from God furnishes the firmest foundation for the stability of the State and public order. At the same time it acts as a curb on the will of the ruler.

It follows that civil obedience does not indicate a slavish mentality but on the contrary must be regarded as an ennobling virtue. Such submission is rational because it implies respect for the will of the Creator from whom all authority flows and because the political superior does not rule us for his sake but for our own fuller good.

Civil authority comprises all power necessary to ensure order and secure the common welfare. It is limited by its purpose and the State can impose no duties that are not related to the common good. Governments are also subject to the moral law and are bound to respect the inalienable rights of individuals. A government that holds itself subject to the dictates of the moral law and refuses to violate the rights of the citizens is built on an impregnable basis. Disregard of right and justice undermines the authority of the State and leads to its downfall. Men will honor and obey a government which truly proves to be a bulwark of justice and is faithful to its task of protecting their highest temporal interests.

3. SCOPE OF CIVIL AUTHORITY

In this question the defect of Liberalism and the excess of Socialism must be avoided. The purpose of government is not merely repression and coercion but also direction. It has a positive and constructive office to perform which consists in furthering the general welfare of the community. This temporal welfare must not be understood merely in material terms but interpreted to embrace the intellectual, cultural, and moral aspects of life insomuch as they bear on man's temporal good and happiness.

Some philosophers, among whom are Kant and Spencer, assign to the State a mere policing activity, confining itself to the protection of rights and the prevention of disorder. Important as this function is, it constitutes only the very minimum of State activity, and no State accepts these narrow limits. Thus Sir Paul Vinogradoff observes: "It may be said at once that the aims of the State are not always the same. It is only the minimum requirements that recur under all circumstances. All States and even rudimentary governments aim at protecting their members from outsiders, and to some extent, from the disorderly conduct of fellow citizens. . . . The tendency toward restricting the State is essential to individualistic liberalism and has been expressed in the history of political thought by the *laissez-faire* policy. It is characterized in doctrine by pronouncements like that of Thomas Paine, that government is a necessary evil. . . . In practice, however, there are no States which hold themselves strictly within the limits of negative protection. All historical commonwealths attend more or less to the positive requirements of their subjects — to their welfare."[1] When we reject this too restricted conception of the office of the State, we do not wish to be understood as giving approval to an equally objectionable State paternalism which injects itself into all private affairs and attempts to regulate all the details of the life of its citizens. The general service which the State should render is to afford opportunities which enable the citizens to exert their own initiative and enterprise in the pursuit of their welfare. A workable rule for State activity is laid down by Cronin in *The Science of Ethics:* "The measure of State function, is to be found in the necessities of man and the inability of the individual and the family to provide these necessities. Anything, therefore, which is necessary whether for the individual or for society at large, and which the individual or the family is not in a position to supply, may legitimately be regarded as included in the end of the State."

4. SERVICES OF THE STATE

All individuals and all legitimate associations have a claim to protection by the State in the pursuit of their ends. Legislation, therefore, must be enacted which safeguards all lawful interests and prevents all forms of exploitation. In order effectually to protect lawful interests the State must build up such organized power which will be strong enough to suppress lawless agencies which prey on the law-abiding portion of the community. Under a weak government injustice

[1] Vinogradoff, P., *Outlines of Historical Jurisprudence*, Oxford Univ. Press, N. Y., p. 93.

abounds and the violators of the law prosper. Activities to be curbed are unfair competition, intimidation, unreasonable boycotts, monopolistic business practices, fraudulent advertising, abuse of the freedom of the press, subversive propaganda, and literature calculated to harm religion and corrupt morals.

Under the positive services come: public works such as control of currency, postal service, water supply, road construction, conservation of natural resources; public education by fostering educational institutions, museums, libraries, and experiment stations; welfare work, public sanitation; improvement of public morality; social legislation. These services are briefly indicated by Suarez: "The object of civil legislation is the natural welfare of the community and of its individual members, in order that they may live in peace and justice, with a sufficiency of those goods that are necessary for the physical conservation and comfort, and with those moral conditions which are required for private well-being and public prosperity."

Whilst the State is interested in education and bound to promote it, the right to educate the children is primarily the right of the parents. Hence, though the State may erect public schools, it has no right to establish a school monopoly.

Again whereas it is on the whole not desirable that the State engage in economic activities, it is entirely within its competence to regulate the economic life and to supervise business in order to secure the public good and to prevent social injustice. It is even the duty of the State to make sure that the wage contract guarantees the laborer a living wage in the full sense of the word. Labor legislation tends to equalize the very unequal condition in which the worker finds himself in respect to the employer and to offset the greater economic power wielded by capital.

5. THE STATE NOT AN END IN ITSELF

The State is not a thing abstracted and distinct from and

superior to the people who compose it. It is not, as Hegel would have it, the Incarnation of the World Spirit nor the Embodiment of Universal Reason. Such deification of the State leads to intolerable consequences. The sovereignty of the State is not unlimited. It is neither a personality nor has it a will of its own. The good of the State, therefore, must be related to the good of the citizens and emphatically we assert that the citizens are not for the State but that the State is for the citizens. The State has no right to demand absolute and blind obedience; it is not the universal conscience, nor the supreme interpreter of morality.

6. THE ORIGIN OF SOVEREIGNTY

In the last analysis, sovereignty is derived from God because it comprises powers which only God can confer. It is transmitted through the people in whom it originally resides but who cannot exercise it except through an organized government.

The form of the government is determined by historical conditions or reasons of expediency.

When a government no longer realizes the ends for which it exists, it forfeits its reason to be and the people can withdraw the authority they have conferred. The tyrannical abuse of power destroys the right to continue to rule. The great evils incident on rebellion, that is, violent overthrow of the government, make the people hesitate to resort to this means and incline them patiently to suffer temporary wrongs. The people will take the grave step of revolution only when all other means of redress have been exhausted and no other hope of deliverance from odious oppression remains.

7. THE DIGNITY OF THE STATE

Whilst we uncompromisingly oppose the Hegelian apotheosis of the State and all forms of State worship, we willingly admit the lofty character and elevated mission of the

State. The majesty of the State shines forth in the greatest splendor, when civil authority makes itself the instrument of justice, the avenger of injustice, and the faithful agency of the common good. The ideal State should be the concrete expression of the right order and the means of the realization of the good life as far as it can be actualized in this world. It should be the embodiment of justice and the harmonization of all interests. States should be deeply imbued with a sense of responsibility and feel that they are only the temporary representatives of something that is greater than they.

The dignity of the State lies in its instrumental value. If not a person in itself, it is the condition of the full personal and unhampered life of its citizens. It is the apparatus by which the individual works out his destiny. It produces the ethical environment necessary for the personal life and its task is to render the social environment ever more ethical. The State is the friend of the individual, securing for him that sacred sphere of individual liberty which, if not thus protected, would soon be profaned and vanish. If individuals were left to themselves, they would really not leave each other to themselves; one would encroach on the other, and no one would have the opportunity of ethical self-realization. Freedom is impossible without order and law. Order is a blessing. Anarchy a curse. The law is a restraint on the evil minded. The ethical value of the State consists in this, that it is the vehicle and matrix of the personal life of its citizens.

In a democratic state, it becomes the duty of the citizens to take active part in the political life of the nation and to exert a wholesome influence on the orientation of governmental policies. The franchise is not merely a privilege but also a very solemn duty. Where government is representative, the citizens are responsible for its moral character and its actions. The neglect of civic duties on the part of the more enlightened members of the community may result in great evil and, accordingly, must be regarded as a moral offense.

Corrupt government is due to the blameworthy apathy of the citizens.

The flag is the symbol of the authority of the State and as such is entitled to proper respect. Demonstrative flag waving is not necessarily a guarantee of genuine patriotism but a good citizen will duly honor the national banner in the customary way.

The State enjoys coercive power in its full extent because its office is to enforce rights and to preserve order. Since there always are individuals who will not obey the law from rational motives, force must be used and punishment inflicted to deter them from violating the law and disturbing the peace. For the sake of order the State has been granted by the supreme Ruler of the universe the right to inflict capital punishment when such a drastic penalty becomes necessary. This is the exclusive prerogative of the sovereign State and imparts to it an august majesty. Punishment should be proportioned to the crime and justly and impartially administered. Whenever possible it should be medicinal and reformative aiming at the rehabilitation of the delinquent. Its chief function is to act as a deterrent from wrongdoing.

8. COSMOPOLITANISM

Loyalty to the State is called patriotism, which though it may be perverted, is a fine human trait. It does not exclude proper respect for other States nor loyalty to our common race. Mankind in general is too abstract an entity to evoke any strong emotional resonance or to lead to any practical activity. A nebulous cosmopolitanism or a specious universal philanthropy is no substitute for devotion to our country. The larger loyalties presuppose the minor loyalties. Patriotism will retain its value even after all national antagonism has been resolved into universal harmony. Cosmopolitanism often is used as an escape from duties which allegiance to the country would impose. He who boasts of his will to serve humanity does so mostly to dispense himself from serving his immediate neighborhood. Humanity becomes my neighbor in my fellow citizen; if I do nothing for him, it is unlikely that I will do anything for humanity. Love of humanity is a convenient virtue because ordinarily it can find no practical expression and remains in the realm of pure sentiment. Thus, we express a genuine love for humanity by serving our country, our community, our family, and our friends. In this manner the all too vague love of humanity becomes concrete and effective and descends to earth from the regions of the clouds. Good citizenship, a broad fraternal charity, an honest and worthy affection for one's family are the best evidence that one's duty to humanity is abundantly fulfilled. Hence patriotism is not only a most praiseworthy social virtue but its absence indicates a character wanting one of the most conspicuous of human traits.

IX

The Church and the State

1. STATE AND RELIGION

The State must further the religious interests of the people but refrain from any interference with liberty of conscience. In promoting the cause of religion it renders itself an excellent service since religion is the strongest force making for morality and good citizenship. Nothing weakens the State more than religious oppression and persecution. Wherever religion is attacked, the ultimate aim is to rob the people of their rights.

The various religious groups must be allowed full freedom and no attempt must be made in any way to interfere with their religious administration. Religious authority must be respected and the law by which the different ecclesiastical bodies are governed properly upheld. Religious bodies have a right to own property and must be protected in this right. They must in no way be disturbed, but rather effectively assisted, in their charitable, educational, and social activities. Such activities redound to the benefit of the entire community. Modern religious conditions require on the part of the government a policy of tolerance and an attitude of sincere friendliness toward the various existing denominations.

2. AUTONOMY OF THE CHURCH

The Church is not a department or a function of the State

but a society in its own right. In its own sphere it is entitled
to absolute self-government. As custodian of the moral law
it has a right to speak with authority on all social and
economic questions that bear on moral issues. In the field of
education it has a prior right in virtue of its divine mission
to teach all peoples of the earth. The State, however, is also
interested in the proper education of its citizens and has the
right to make the necessary provisions for this purpose.
Hence Pius XI says in the encyclical on the *Christian Education of Youth:* "The State can exact, and take measures to
secure that all its citizens have the necessary knowledge of
their civic and political duties, and a certain degree of physical, intellectual, and moral culture, which, considering the
conditions of our times, is really essential to the common
good."

To live under the diarchy of Church and State serves the
best interests of the people, offers the strongest guarantee of
human liberty and stands out as an impregnable bulwark
against all forms of totalitarianism. Throughout the centuries the Church has fought the battles of the people against
oppression.

X

The Family of Nations

---

1. JUSTICE BETWEEN STATES

The relations between States must also be governed by justice and charity because States, though sovereign, are not above the moral law. At present international relations are in a chaotic condition, but there is a growing movement to place them on a solid judicial basis. President Wilson declared in 1917: "We are at the beginning of an age in which it will be insisted that the same standards of conduct and responsibility for wrong done shall be observed among the nations and their governments that are observed among individual citizens of civilized states." To bring mankind nearer to this consummation it will be necessary to devise appropriate machinery for the purpose of administering justice and settling disputes between the nations.

2. A SOCIETY OF NATIONS

Organized humanity will most likely not take the form of a superstate but rather of a federation of equal nations pledged to respect each other's rights and to cooperate in the interests of a common civilization. Association between men extends on an ever broadening basis and will finally embrace the whole race. Thus Dr. John Eppstein writes: "It is nature itself, that eloquent interpreter of the Divine Will, which calls all people to form among themselves one universal association and at the same time makes it their duty to do so! In this manner does Taparelli d'Azeglio express the logical conclusion of a process of reasoning which his predecessors in Christian philosophy had advanced. If man is essentially social, and if history proves the smaller society, from household to State, to have need of the greater, is there any reason to suppose that the process of social organization must end at the State?"[1] The old Christian concept of the solidarity of the human race is beginning again to assert itself.

3. WAR

Modern warfare has become so ruinous that a war is dreaded by all sane nations and statesmen regard the prevention of war as one of their most solemn duties. The old-time glorification of war has ceased and war has been stripped of its glamour. The theory that war is a biological necessity or "an essential element in God's scheme of the world" is violently repudiated. War is rather looked on as sheer folly, inane futility, and stark madness. An aggressive war would be considered as a crime against humanity. The Kellogg pact renounces war as an instrument of national policy. The day may not be far off when war will be completely outlawed. War may be the law of the jungle, it cannot be the law of humanity for in the end it would prove a suicidal policy. In the nation its action is highly dysgenic and in the world it is destructive of incalculable cultural values. Pertinently Prof. Carver remarks in *Essays in Social Justice:* "That the meek shall inherit the earth is probably a scientific statement." Exaggerated nationalism and chauvinistic patriotism (jingoism) are a perpetual menace to world peace. With regard to these unwholesome manifestations of a noble sentiment Lord Hugh Cecil says: "What is needed is to realize that nationalism is not a quasi religion, as some people seem almost to imagine, but a human passion, like other passions beneficent only so long as it is strictly disci-

[1] *The Catholic Tradition of the Law of Nations*, p. 247.

plined and controlled by the moral law, mischievous and debasing so soon as it passes beyond that control. Nationalism
is like the passion of acquisition or the sex passion. Within
the limits which moralists have long ago assigned to them,
these passions are beneficent; they are, indeed, the mainspring of a very large part of human action."[2] He does not
truly love his country who fosters within it national egotism,
an unwarranted consciousness of superiority, imperialism,
and the spirit of martial aggressiveness. Any real international partnership will demand from the citizens of all
nations, not less patriotism, but a stronger and loftier patriotism; not the blind and selfish patriotism which desires
only national aggrandizement and national gain, but that far
purer love of country which would fain see it play its part
in some real international partnership and make its own
special contribution to the common good of the whole world.

In the world of today the only war that can be justified is
a defensive war. Such a war may be thrust upon a peace-
loving people by a warlike neighbor. In its justification
Suarez says: "Defensive war is not only licit, but it is sometimes even a duty. It is accepted not only by public magis-
trates but also by private persons; for it is always lawful to
repel force by force." But even in war the moral law may not
be set aside and armed conflict must be conducted in a
humane fashion. Though a war affords opportunities for a
display of the finest human qualities, it more frequently un-
looses the basest, vilest, and most brutish instincts in man.

[2] A Letter to the *Times,* Oct., 1921.

XI

The Growth of Moral Sentiment

In spite of temporary setbacks, it may be reasonably asserted that mankind's moral perceptions are constantly becoming clearer, its moral ideals purer, and its sense of moral responsibility stronger and more alert. This is quite apparent in the wide realm of social morality. Practices in political and economic life, formerly fully sanctioned, now incur severe condemnation; great calamities evoke universal sympathy and bring spontaneous response; philanthropy is expanding; sensitiveness to social wrong is becoming more acute and in one way and another men are becoming conscious that they are their brothers' keepers. We not only relieve misery but try to stop its source.

The general moral improvement must be attributed to the leaven of Christianity which is permeating the mass of humanity and raising the moral tone of public life. It was the aim of the new religion of love to build up a kingdom of righteousness and a genuine world fellowship. True, the purpose has not yet been accomplished but the world is moving in the right direction. A writer remarks: "The unaccomplished mission of Christianity is to reconstruct society on the basis of brotherhood." Quite so. But the work is going on.

Everyone feels in his heart that according to the measure of his ability it is his solemn duty to assist in the building of this finer world in which it will be easier for man to work out his destiny, in which there will be fewer obstacles to right living, in which contact with the social environment will be uplifting rather than degrading, in which generous hearts reach out in active sympathy to the poor and distressed, and in which helpful hands guide and steady the faltering brother.

Bibliography

NOTE: This is a survey of the literature of ethics. Books listed here are by no means all recommended.

Adam, D. S., *A Handbook of Christian Ethics* (Edinburgh: Clark).

Adler, F., *An Ethical Philosophy of Life.*

——— *The Reconstruction of the Spiritual Ideal* (New York: Appleton).

Allen, A. B., *The Psychology of Punishment* (London: Allman).

Aristotle, *The Nicomachean Ethics.* Translated by J. E. C. Welldon (New York: Macmillan).

Bentham, J., *An Introduction to the Principles of Morals and Legislation* (Oxford: Clarendon Press).

Bixby, J. Th., *The Crisis in Morals* (Boston: Robert Brothers).

Bowne, P. B., *The Principles of Ethics* (New York: American Book Co.).

Bruehl, C., *Birthcontrol and Eugenics* (New York: Wagner).

——— *The Popes Plan for Social Reconstruction* (New York: Devin-Adair).

Calkins, M. Wh., *The Good Man and the Good* (New York: Macmillan).

Carrel, A., *Man the Unknown* (New York: Harper's).

Castelein, A., *Droit Naturel* (Bruxelles).

Cathrein, V., *Moralphilosophie* (St. Louis: Herder).

——— *Die Einheit des sittlichen Bewusstseins der Menschheit* (Herder).

Chesterton, G. K., *What's Wrong with the World* (New York: Dodd, Mead & Co.).

Cooper, J. M., *Birth Control* (Washington: N.C.W.C.).

Coppens, C., *Moral Principles and Medical Practice* (New York: Schwarz, Kirwin and Fauss).

——— *Moral Philosophy.*

Cox, I., *Liberty. Its Use and Abuse* (New York: Fordham University Press).

Cronin, J., *Economics and Society* (New York: American Book Co.).

Cronin, M., *The Science of Ethics* (Dublin: Gill).

Cuthbert, O.S.F.C., *Catholic Ideals in Social Life* (London: Washbourne).

D'Arcy, M. C., *Christian Morals* (New York: Longmans).

Dawson, C., *Religion and the Modern State* (New York: Sheed & Ward).

Day, H. C., *The New Morality* (St. Louis: Herder).

DeHovre, F., *Philosophy and Education*. Transl. by E. B. Jordan (New York: Benziger).

DeLaguna, Th., *Introduction to the Science of Ethics* (New York: Macmillan).

Deploige, S., *The Conflict Between Ethics and Sociology*. Transl. by C. C. Miltner (St. Louis: Herder).

Dewey, J., and Tufts, J. H., *Ethics* (New York: Holt).

Dixon, W. M., *The Human Situation* (New York: Longmans).

Drake, Durant, *The New Morality* (New York: Macmillan).

Dresser, H. W., *Ethics. Its Theory and Application* (New York: Crowel).

Driesch, H., *Ethical Principles* (New York: Norton).

Dubois, P., *Self-Control and How to Secure It* (New York: Funk & Wagnalls).

Ellwood, C. A., *The Reconstruction of Religion* (New York: Macmillan).

Encyclopedia of the Social Sciences (New York: Macmillan).

Encyclopedia of Religion and Ethics (New York: Scribner's Sons).

Encyclopedia, The Catholic (New York).

Eppstein, J., *The Catholic Tradition of the Law of Nations* (Washington, D. C.: Catholic Association for International Peace).

Fairbairn, A. M., *The Philosophy of the Christian Religion* (New York: Macmillan).

Fallon, V., *Principles of Social Economy* (New York: Benziger).

Farrell, W., *A Companion to the Summa* (New York: Sheed & Ward).

Fite, W., *An Introduction to the Study of Ethics* (New York: Longmans).

Foerster, F. W., *Marriage and the Sex-Problem*. Transl. by M. Booth (New York: Stokes).

—— *Schuld und Suehne* (Munich).

Fox, J. J., *Religion and Morality* (New York: Young).

Furfey, P., *Three Theories of Society* (New York: Macmillan).

Galloway, Th. W., *The Use of Motives in Teaching Morals and Religion* (Boston: Pilgrim Press).

Geis, R., *Principles of Catholic Sex Morality.* Transl. by C. Bruehl (New York: Wagner).

Geisert, H. A., *The Criminal* (St. Louis: Herder).

Glenn, P. J., *Ethics* (St. Louis: Herder).

Hadfield, J. A., *Psychology and Morals* (New York: McBride).

Hamilton, E. J., *The Moral Law or the Theory and the Practice of Duty* (New York: Funk and Wagnalls).

Hardman, O., *The Ideals of Asceticism* (New York: Macmillan).

Hartmann, N., *Ethics.* Transl. by Stanton Coit (New York: Macmillan).

Hatch, W., *The Moral Philosophy of Aristotle* (London: Murray).

Hayes, C. J., *Essays on Nationalism* (New York: Macmillan).

Hayes, E., *Sociology and Ethics* (New York: Appleton).

Hill, Owen A., *Ethics: General and Special* (New York: Macmillan).

Hill, W. H., *Ethics or Moral Philosophy* (Baltimore: Murphy).

Hobhouse, L. T., *Morals in Evolution* (New York: Holt).

Hollaind, R., *Natural Law and Legal Practice* (New York: Benziger).

Hull, E. R., *The Formation of Character* (St. Louis: Herder).

—— *Why Should I Be Moral?* (New York: Kenedy).

Humphrey, W., *Conscience and Law* (London: Baker).

Husslein, J., *Social Wellsprings* (Milwaukee: Bruce).

Jacks, M. L., *God in Education* (London: Rich and Cowan).

James, W., *Memories and Studies* (New York: Longmans).

—— *The Principles of Psychology* (New York: Holt).

—— *The Varieties of Religious Experience* (New York: Longmans).

Janet, P., *The Theory of Morals* (New York: Scribner's Sons).

Joad, C. E. M., *Return to Philosophy* (New York: Dutton & Co.).

Johnston, G. A., *An Introduction to Ethics* (New York: Macmillan).

Kalmer, L., and Meyer, J., *Crime and Religion* (Chicago: Franciscan Herald).

Kane, R., *Worth* (New York: Longmans).

Kant's *Critique of Practical Reason*. Transl. by Thomas Kingsmill Abbott (New York: Longmans).

Keane, H., *A Primer of Moral Philosophy* (New York: Kenedy).

Kerby, W. J., *The Social Mission of Charity* (New York: Macmillan).

Koch, A., *A Handbook of Moral Theology*. Transl. by A. Preuss (St. Louis: Herder).

Ladd, G. T., *Philosophy of Conduct* (New York: Scribner's Sons).

——— *What Ought I to Do?* (New York: Longmans).

Laski, H. J., *Authority in the Modern State*.

——— *Studies in the Problem of Sovereignty* (New Haven: Yale University Press).

Lecky, W. E. H., *History of European Morals* (New York: Appleton).

Leibell, J., *Readings in Ethics* (Chicago: Loyola University Press).

Leo XIII, *The Great Encyclical Letters* (New York: Benziger).

LeRoy, A., *The Religion of the Primitives* (New York: Macmillan).

Lilly, W. S., *On Right and Wrong* (London: Chapman & Hall).

Lindworsky, J., *The Training of the Will* (Milwaukee: Bruce).

Link, H. C., *The Return to Religion* (New York: Macmillan).

Lockington, W. J., *Bodily Health and Spiritual Vigor* (New York: Longmans).

Lowie, R. H., *Primitive Society* (New York: Boni and Liveright).

Mackenzie, J. S., *Manual of Ethics* (New York: Noble).

MacGrath, M. C., *A Study of the Moral Development of Children* (Princeton, N. J.).

Mallock, W. H., *Is Life Worth Living?* (New York: Putnam's).

Martineau, J., *Types of Ethical Theory* (New York: Macmillan).

McDonald, W., *Principles of Moral Science* (Dublin: Gill).

Mercier, D., *A Manual of Modern Scholastic Philosophy* (London).

Mezes, S. E., *Ethics: Descriptive and Explanatory* (New York: Macmillan).

Mill, J. S., *Utilitarianism. Liberty and Representative Government* (New York: Dutton).

Miltner, C. C., *The Elements of Ethics* (New York: Macmillan).

Ming, J. J., *The Data of Modern Ethics Examined* (New York: Benziger).

Moore, G. E., *Ethics* (New York: Holt).

Moore, Th. V., *A Historical Introduction to Ethics* (New York: American Book Co.).

——— *Principles of Ethics* (Philadelphia: Lippincott).

——— *The Physical Factors in Crime* (Washington: N.C.W.C.).

Morrison, Bakewell, *Marriage* (Milwaukee: Bruce).

Muirhead, J. H., *The Elements of Ethics* (New York: Scribner's Sons).

Muntsch, A., and Spalding, H. S., *Introductory Sociology* (New York: Heath).

Murray, R. W., *Introductory Sociology* (New York: Crofts).

Neumann, H., *Education for Moral Growth* (New York: Appleton).

——— *Modern Youth and Marriage* (New York: Appleton).

Payot, J., *The Conquest of Happiness* (New York: Funk and Wagnalls).

——— *The Education of the Will* (New York: Funk and Wagnalls).

Paulsen, F., *A System of Ethics*. Transl. by F. Thilly (New York: Scribner's Sons).

Pius XI, *On Christian Marriage.*

——— *On Christian Education.*

——— *On Atheistic Communism.*

——— *Quadragesimo Anno.*

Pius XII, *Summi Pontificatus.*

Poland, W., *Fundamentals of Ethics* (New York: Silver, Burdett & Co.).

Rashdall, H., *Is Conscience an Emotion?* (New York: Houghton, Mifflin & Co.).

Rauschenbusch, W., *Christianizing the Social Order* (New York: Macmillan).

Rickaby, J., *Moral Philosophy* (New York: Longmans).

——— *Aquinas Ethicus* (New York: Benziger).

——— *Political and Moral Essays* (New York: Benziger).

Ritchie, D. G., *Natural Rights* (New York: Macmillan).

Rogers, A. K., *The Theory of Ethics* (New York: Macmillan).

Rogers, R. A. P., *A Short History of Ethics* (New York: Macmillan).

Ross, E. J., *A Survey of Sociology* (Milwaukee: Bruce).

Ross, J. Elliot, *Ethics from the Standpoint of Scholastic Philosophy* (New York: Devin-Adair).

Ross, Sir W. D., *Foundations of Ethics* (Oxford: Clarendon Press).

Royce, J., *The Philosophy of Loyalty* (New York: Macmillan).

Ryan, J. A., *Distributive Justice* (New York: Macmillan).

Ryan, J. A., and Miller, M., *State and Church* (New York: Macmillan).

Salsmans, J., *Droit et Morale* (Bruges).

Schlick, M., *Problems of Ethics*. Transl. by David Rynin (New York: Prentice Hall).

Schmidt, W., *The Origin and Growth of Religion* (New York: Mac Veagh).

Schwer, W., *Catholic Social Theory*. Transl. by B. Landheer (St. Louis: Herder).

Selbie, W. B., *The Psychology of Religion* (Oxford: Clarendon Press).

Seth, J., *A Study of Ethical Principles* (New York: Scribner's Sons).

Sharp, F. C., *Ethics* (New York: Century Co.).

Sheen, F. J., *The Moral Universe* (Milwaukee: Bruce).

―――― *Freedom Under God* (Milwaukee: Bruce).

Sidgwick, H., *The Methods of Ethics* (New York: Macmillan).

Slater, Th., *Religion and Human Interests* (New York: Benziger).

Small, A. W., *General Sociology* (Chicago: University Press).

Snowden, J. H., *The Psychology of Religion* (New York: Revell).

Sorley, W. R., *Moral Values and the Idea of God* (Cambridge: Gifford Lectures).

Sortais, G., *Traite de Philosophie* (Paris).

Spalding, J. L., *Glimpses of Truth* (Chicago: MacClurg & Co.).

Spencer, A., *The Family and Its Members* (Philadelphia: Lippincott).

Spencer, H., *The Data of Ethics* (New York: Burt).

―――― *The Principles of Ethics* (New York: Appleton).

Sturzo, L., *Church and State* (New York: Longmans).

Sullivan, J., *General Ethics* (Worcester: Holy Cross College Press).

Tawney, R. H., *Religion and the Rise of Capitalism* (New York: Harcourt, Brace & Co.).

Thilly, F., *Introduction to Ethics* (New York; Scribner's Sons).

Thomas Aquinas, *The Summa Theologica*. Transl. by the English Dominicans (New York: Benziger).

Thornton, L. S., *Conduct and the Supernatural* (New York: Longmans).

Thornton, W. Th., *Oldfashioned Ethics and Commonsense Metaphysics* (New York: Macmillan).

Titus, H. H., *Ethics for Today* (New York: American Book Co.).

Tufts, J. H., *Our Democracy. Its Origins and Its Tasks* (New York: Holt).

Vann, G., *Morals Makyth Man* (New York: Longmans).

Vinogradoff, Sir Paul, *Outlines of Historical Jurisprudence* (Oxford: University Press).

Von Nell-Breuning, O., *Reorganization of Society*. Transl. by B. W. Dempsey (Milwaukee: Bruce).

Von Streng, F., *Marriage*. Transl. by C. Bruehl (New York: Benziger).

Walsh, J. J., *Religion and Health* (Boston: Little, Brown & Co.).

Westermark, E., *Origins and Development of the Moral Ideas* (New York: Macmillan).

——— *The Future of Marriage in Western Civilization* (New York: Macmillan).

Wheelwright, P., *A Critical Introduction to Ethics* (Garden City, N. Y.: Doubleday).

Wiley, Th., E., *Community Structure* (St. Louis: Herder).

Willigan, W. L., and O'Connor, J. J., *Sociology* (New York: Longmans).

Windle, Sir Bertram C. A., *Science and Morals* (London: Burns & Oates).

Wittmann, M., *Ethik* (Munich).

Woods, E. S., *Every-Day Religion* (New York: Macmillan).

Woods, H., *First Book in Ethics* (New York: Wagner).

Wundt, W., *Facts of the Moral Life* (New York: Macmillan).

Index

social value of religion, 166

La Rochefoucauld, on hypocrisy, 5

Law, natural, 120; positive, 123

Laws, penal, 123

Lecky, W. E. H., on distinction between good and bad, 108

Leo XIII, on family, 212; on positive law, 123; on propertyless class, 204; on public worship, 164

Le Roy, A., Bishop, on morality of primitives, 99

Lessing, G. E., on dignity of work, 184

Life, probationary, 42; relative character of, 42

Love, a will to help, 190

Lubbock, Sir J., on primitives, 99

Lying, evil consequences of, 195; intrinsically evil, 194

MacKenzie, J. S., on conventions, 107; on practical character of ethics, 14

Man, citizen of a spiritual world, 45; dignity of, 44; his destiny, 38 f.; never mere means, 145; not guided by instinct, 16; social nature of, 209; virtuous, 139

Maritain, J., on ideal of life, 22

Marriage, properties of, 211

Martin, E. D., on unsatisfactoriness of life, 41

Mental cruelty, 192

Mercier, D. Cardinal, on eternal sanctions, 131

Merit, 129

Mill, J. S., on utilitarianism, 80

Moore, Dom Th. V., on a plan of life, 17; on profession, 185

Moral act, 60 ff.

Moral agent, 47 ff.

Moral character, 138

Moral education and religion, 33

Moral intuitionism, 88

Moral judgment, 87 ff.

Moral law, 117 ff.

Moral life, unity of, 159

Moral notions, 98 ff.

Moral order, 108 ff.

Moral sanctions, 128 ff.

Moral training, 21

Morality, and religion, 33, 167; as a

fact, 3; as a force, 6; as experience, 5; as sentiment, 7; in language, 4; conform to nature, 110; derived from object, 62; independent, 31; is beneficial, 113; modern, 102; norm of, 110; not hostile to progress, 45; not merely restraint, 19; religious, 31; social, 205 ff.; traditional, 101; unreflective, 17

Morality and happiness, 35

Morality and theism, 25

Mores, 4, 13

Motivations, moral, 23

Muirhead, J. H., on conscience, 93

Nationalism, 225

Natural law, 120 ff.

Norm, ultimate of morality, 114

Obedience, civil, 214

Objective moral order, 62

Optimism, 170

Order, International, 224

Ought, moral, 90, 119

Ownership, private, reasons for, 200 ff.; wide diffusion of, 204

Pain, function of, 76

Passions, 52

Paternalism, 216

Patience, 142

Patriotism, 220

Paulsen, F., on object of ethics, 12; on unkindness, 193

Perjury, 195

Personality and character, 138

Pessimism, 170

Pius XI, on economic exploitation, 115; on justice and charity, 154; on intrinsical wrong, 66; on modification of wage contract, 204; on moral import of economics, 27; on proper recreation, 76; on public ownership, 203; on State and education, 223

Pius XII, on human rights, 146; on universal norm of morality, 18

Play and character development, 73

Playgrounds and juvenile delinquency, 75

Pleasure, as criterion of morality, 79; good of lower order, 68; pursuit